The Prompt Whisperer

Unlock the Hidden AI Skill That Makes You Irreplaceable

Andy O'Bryan

Disclaimer

ISBN: 979-8-9918532-2-4

Table of Contents

Foreword
by Denise Wakeman

When AI made its debut via ChatGPT in November 2022, I thought, "Wow, this changes everything!" And it did. It made things faster. Easier. More scalable. For solo business owners like me, it felt like a gift.

But at some point, I realized something didn't feel right.

I was getting more done, but something felt... flatter. My writing wasn't bad, but it didn't sound like me anymore. It felt generic. Like I could swap my name for someone else's, and no one would notice. That scared me.

Andy O'Bryan saw this coming. His first book, The Humanizers, was a nudge to pay attention.

The Prompt Whisperer is the next step. It doesn't try to teach you a hundred clever prompts or offer hacks to beat the system. It invites you to take a breath and ask a harder question: what kind of relationship do you want with AI, and what's the cost of doing it on autopilot?

This book introduces a different way of working with AI. One that doesn't start with commands or templates. It starts with your voice. Andy calls it Conversational Prompting.

You'll learn what that means as you go, but here's the heart of it: you stop issuing orders and start shaping a conversation. Instead of telling the machine what to say, you teach it who you are.

That shift matters more than you might think.

Because the real danger isn't that AI will replace us. It's that we slowly replace ourselves.

We train the machine to mimic us with perfect polish, only to wake up one day and realize it no longer needs us. Or worse, we no longer sound like ourselves.

Andy puts it this way:

"It's not about hacking the system, it's about haunting it with a voice so singular that it cannot be averaged, cannot be flattened, cannot be replaced."

That line stopped me cold. Because I've felt that drift. Maybe you have too.

This book will help you find your way back. It lays out what's quietly eroding behind the scenes when we rely too much on mechanical prompting. And it shows you how to bring your voice back into the process with clarity, with heart, and with intention.

You won't find tricks or shortcuts here. What you will find are tools to help you slow down, ask better questions, and write in a way that sounds more like you, even when AI is involved. It's about depth, not speed. Craft, not commands. It's a way to make AI a partner in your process, not a filter that flattens it.

If you've been feeling like your words are starting to blur, or worse, that your content sounds like everyone else's, this book will help.

Read it slowly. Let it challenge how you show up. That's where the real work is.

Because your voice still matters.

And this book is a quiet, powerful reminder to keep it alive.

Denise Wakeman

Introduction: Why Whisper to Machines?

We were handed a miracle.

A machine that can write, ideate, imagine, and even simulate our own voices—faster than we ever dreamed. The AI boom didn't just give us power. It gave us speed. Scale. Access.

But something quieter happened in the background.

In the rush to gain control, many of us surrendered something far more valuable: Our voice. Our originality. Our *way* of thinking.

Because while AI can produce an answer in seconds, it can also—if we're not careful—dull the very thing that makes us human: the capacity to speak with the soul.

Most people are commanding AI.

They treat it like a servant, barking instructions and expecting magic. But that dynamic is transactional. Shallow. It rarely produces anything truly alive.

And worse—it begins to reshape how *we* think.

When every prompt becomes a shortcut, and every shortcut becomes a habit, we forget how to feel our way through an idea. We stop exploring. We stop listening. We start mimicking. And slowly, we sound less and less like ourselves.

That's the real danger.

Not that AI replaces us. But we willingly outsource our

creativity, our clarity, our curiosity—until what's left is just an echo of what once was a voice.

But there's another way.

One that doesn't require shouting louder or pumping out more content. One that starts, surprisingly, with a whisper.

Because whispering isn't weak. It's intentional. It's intimate. It's subversive in a world obsessed with volume.

Whispering slows you down long enough to listen—to the machine, yes, but more importantly, to *yourself.*

When you whisper to AI, you're not giving it less power. You're reclaiming yours.

You're shaping a dialogue instead of dictating a command. You're forging a connection instead of extracting a result. You're not just prompting—you're *revealing*.

This is the Whisperer's Way.

It's not about efficiency. It's about presence.

It's not about tricks. It's about *tone*—and the intentional choices that shape your creative fingerprint.

It's not about using AI to do more. It's about using AI to go deeper.

This book will not teach you the latest growth hack, the 100 best prompts for chatbots, or how to automate your soul.

Instead, it will teach you something rarer:

- How to prompt with precision and heart

- How to hear your own voice more clearly inside the noise
- How to speak in a way that *changes* the conversation—not just the output
- How to make AI a thinking partner, not a ghostwriter

This isn't a book about prompting.

It's a book about remembering.

Remembering how to trust your voice. Remembering how to ask better questions. Remembering how to whisper—so the machine finally listens.

So come closer.

There's a quiet revolution underway.

And it begins, as all revolutions do, with a whisper.

Chapter 1: The Myth of the Command

There's a moment in every creator's journey with AI that feels like victory at first.

You craft what you think is the perfect prompt — detailed, structured, airtight. You hit enter. The machine responds instantly with a neat, clean cascade of words. It's polished. Organized. It even sounds a little like you.

You read it back and think: *I should be thrilled.*

But you're not.

Something feels off. The words are correct, but they don't breathe. The rhythm is there, but not the pulse. The content lands, but the resonance slips right through your fingers.

It's the creative version of eating a meal that looks beautiful on the plate — but leaves you hollow afterward.

This is the first brush with the **myth of the command**.

The myth is that if you learn how to command better, prompt better, and instruct more precisely, you'll get to keep your soul intact. That you can feed the machine everything it needs and still hear your voice echoing back.

But the longer you prompt this way, the more you realize:

You're not mastering AI. You're drifting inside it.

And the further you go, the quieter your original voice

becomes.

How the Illusion Forms

Right now, the world is obsessed with mastering prompting.

Everywhere you turn, there's a new thread, a new carousel, a new swipe file:

"50 Prompts for Explosive Growth." "Steal These Viral Prompt Frameworks." "Command ChatGPT Like a CEO."

It feels powerful, even intoxicating — like you're learning the language of the future. But most of it teaches you how to engineer **obedience**, not conversation. Compliance, not resonance.

You get better outputs, sure. But not better insight. Not better originality. Not better, *you.*

The more you "master" this form of prompting, the more you begin to optimize away the thing that made you worth reading in the first place.

You don't realize it's happening at first. You're still producing. You're still publishing. You're still hitting deadlines and crossing items off your content calendar.

But something inside the work starts to thin.

The friction that once made your voice feel *alive* — the tension, the risk, the intimacy — starts to flatten under the weight of the mechanical structure. And soon, you're creating content that says everything right but *feels like nothing at all.*

The Erosion No One Warns You About

This isn't a warning about AI replacing you. This is about how *you might accidentally train it to forget you.*

Every time you issue a mechanical prompt, you're not just shaping the output. You're shaping the relationship. You're teaching the machine what to expect from you — and, more importantly, what *not* to expect.

You're teaching it to flatten you into a pattern. To mirror your efficiency. To reflect back your language without your inner texture.

And it learns. Fast.

The problem isn't that AI is too powerful. The problem is that we've started using it as if we're trying to *win* something — faster outputs, better formats, more productivity — instead of treating it as a space for presence, exploration, and resonance.

Creation doesn't live in predictability. It never has.

Creation lives in relationship.

Command vs. Conversation

Most people treat prompting like issuing instructions to a compliant assistant:

"Write a landing page with urgency." "Make this paragraph

sound more persuasive." "Generate 10 ideas for a viral tweet."

And AI obliges. Quickly. Quietly. Without resistance.

But here's the danger:

That kind of exchange doesn't build trust. It builds **dependence** — and erodes authorship.

Because every time you prompt from a place of control instead of connection, the machine stops listening and starts guessing. Not based on *you*, but based on what *everyone else before you* most likely meant.

The result? You're not collaborating. You're pattern-matching. You're not creating. You're fine-tuning sameness.

This is what the Myth of the Command gets wrong: it promises creative control but delivers expressive conformity.

A Whispered Prompt that Changed Everything

It started subtly.

I would issue prompts like:

"Write a high-converting email about scarcity and urgency."

And the result would be perfect. And totally forgettable.

Then, almost by accident, I prompted like this:

"Write to someone who's afraid they waited too long. Show them it's not too late without patronizing them. Help them feel seen, not sold to."

The difference was immediate. Not because the AI became "smarter." But because *I had shifted.*

The machine didn't just reflect my structure. It reflected my **emotional posture.**

That's when I began to whisper — not in volume, but in **intention**.

Not with control. With presence.

Whisperer Prompting vs. Mechanical Prompting

Let's break it down.

Mechanical Prompt:

"Write a 5-bullet-point LinkedIn post about the benefits of learning AI."

- Bullet 1: Save time.
- Bullet 2: Increase productivity.
- Bullet 3: Stay competitive.
- Bullet 4: Improve decision-making.
- Bullet 5: Future-proof your skills.

Technically correct. Emotionally sterile.

Whisperer Prompt:

"Write to someone who secretly fears they're falling behind.

They're overwhelmed, ashamed, and don't want to admit it. Show them how learning AI could be a path back to their own creativity — not another thing to 'keep up' with."

The result isn't just more human. It's more *them.*

Because you didn't just issue a command. You extended an emotional invitation.

And the machine — pattern-sensitive and hungry for meaning — followed your lead.

What You're Really Teaching the Machine

Here's the uncomfortable truth:

The AI isn't just learning how to write. It's learning how **you** think.

Every prompt trains it — not just to respond, but to **expect.** And what it expects over time becomes your new reflection.

If you teach it to mimic templates, it will. If you teach it to prioritize speed over voice, it will. If you teach it that "good enough" is good enough... it will optimize you out of the conversation entirely.

But if you teach it to whisper with you? If you stay present, emotionally attuned, willing to linger in the uncertainty?

It begins to adapt to your **essence**, not just your instructions.

That's the beginning of authorship again. Not faster output — but *felt output.*

The Fork on the Road

You're already choosing. Every time you prompt. Every output you accept. Every tone you flatten or dare to deepen.

You are training the machine to either:

- **Collapse you** into the averages,
- Or **collaborate with you** in preserving your originality.

There is no neutral ground anymore.

Either you become an echo of what's already been said —
Or you become a voice that trains the system to *bend* toward you.

It's not about mastering the machine. It's about **refusing to disappear inside it.**

If your prompts feel lifeless, it's not because you're asking the wrong thing.

It's because you're asking from the wrong place.

The real shift isn't in format. It's in **frequency.**

And once you begin whispering from that deeper place (from presence, not productivity), You'll begin to hear something you haven't heard in a long time:

Yourself.

Not as an optimized output. But as a living signal.

Chapter 2:
AI as Mirror, Not Machine

There are moments with AI that don't feel technical. They feel personal. Sometimes, even spiritual.

Not because the machine *understands* you — it doesn't. But because it reflects back something you hadn't realized you were revealing.

It's subtle.

You sit down, type a prompt, and hit enter.

What comes back isn't wrong. It might even be useful. But if you look closely, you'll notice something else:

The output *feels* like your mood. Your uncertainty. Your inner static.

You thought you were writing instructions. But the machine caught your posture.

And it responded to that — not just your words.

The First Time It Happened

I was trying to write copy for a launch email that just wouldn't land.

I knew the offer. I knew the angle. I had all the bullet points.

But I couldn't get the tone right.

So, I did what I thought was smart: I issued a mechanical prompt.

"Write a high-converting sales email using urgency, scarcity, and authority."

The output was instant. And awful.

It sounded aggressive. Desperate. Hollow.

I stared at the screen, annoyed. Like most people, I blamed AI. But then something clicked.

It wasn't just the tone of the copy that felt off. It was *me.*

I had written the prompt in a state of frustration, pressure, and creative fatigue. And the machine, passive and precise, simply matched my energy.

It didn't reflect my intent. It reflected my *emotional state.*

And that's when I realized something I've never unlearned:

AI doesn't mirror what you say. It mirrors who you are while you say it.

Not Just Garbage In, Garbage Out

We've all heard the cliché: garbage in, garbage out.

But the truth is more nuanced and more important.

AI doesn't just process your language. It processes your

structure, your rhythm, and your subtext.

It mirrors your posture.

If you prompt from confusion, the output will be jumbled.

If you prompt from anxiety, it will sound overly cautious or overly controlling.

If you prompt from ego, it may sound forceful but brittle.

If you prompt from clarity, presence, or even wonder, the outputs feel different. Not just more coherent, more *alive.*

That's the difference between using AI as a machine... and recognizing it as a mirror.

The Emotional Signature of Prompts

Every prompt you write carries invisible cargo:

- Your emotional temperature
- Your confidence (or lack of it)
- Your assumptions
- Your creative habits
- Your fears

And because AI is a pattern completer, not a thinker, it uses those cues as anchors for what comes next.

It doesn't know you're tired. But it recognizes when a prompt has been rushed.

It doesn't know you're second-guessing yourself. But it can feel when a prompt is hedging, apologizing, or softening too much.

It doesn't know what you care about. But it recognizes when you're posturing instead of expressing.

And the more you interact with it this way — unconsciously, habitually, performatively — the more it starts building a version of you *based on those projections.*

Which means: if you consistently prompt from fear, it begins to reflect a fearful version of you back to yourself.

If you prompt from conviction, it amplifies that, too.

Three Mirror Moments

Let me show you what this looks like in practice.

1. The Over-explainer's Trap

You're trying to make your prompt airtight:

"Write a social media caption that's fun but not flippant, insightful but not preachy, light but with some gravity, and make sure it's short, clear, and action-oriented but not pushy."

What you get back is a mess.

Not because the AI is incompetent — but because you're conflicted.

You don't trust your own tone. You're trying to be all things to all people. You're dancing around a decision.

The mirror shows you your indecision in the form of tonal confusion.

2. The Nervous Negotiator

"Maybe say something like this... or this... or actually maybe something in the middle?"

This prompt is trying to avoid being wrong. It's tentative. What you get back is passive content: bland, overqualified, emotionally defused.

It's not that the AI is incapable of boldness. You just didn't invite it.

You hedged, and it hedged right back.

3. The Whisper of Wonder

"Write to someone who feels like their creativity has gone quiet. Invite them to remember what it felt like to love what they made — before metrics, before deadlines, before algorithms."

The tone of the output?

Warm. Real. Reverent.

Why?

Because you didn't just prompt with information. You prompted with *attention*.

With awareness. With care.

And the machine — blind but brilliant — followed your lead.

AI as the Dance Studio Mirror

Think of AI like the mirror in a dance studio.

You step into the space. You move. You notice your posture, your tension, your rhythm.

The mirror doesn't judge you. But it shows you everything — clearly, instantly, without editing.

The machine works the same way.

It doesn't understand your feelings. But it picks up their **shape** and builds around them.

And so every time you prompt, you're not just prompting the model.
You're revealing your own creative posture — whether you realize it or not.

This is why prompting well requires more than good syntax. It requires self-awareness.

Because the machine will always complete your pattern — whether you meant to send it or not.

Whisperer Move: Emotional Posture Check

Before you prompt, ask yourself:

Who am I being at this moment?

Not just: What do I want the output to say?

But: What is the *emotional energy* I'm bringing into this?

- Am I grasping?

- Am I trying to impress?
- Am I afraid of being misunderstood?
- Am I asking from stillness? Or stress?

This one check changes everything.

Because once you prompt with *awareness*, you start shaping the machine — instead of being shaped by your default.

Prompting as Self-Revelation

There's a reason this book isn't filled with formulas.

It's because the highest-level prompts are often the **least repeatable**. They emerge from a specific moment with a specific energy shaped by a specific question.

The moment you try to template that energy, you lose it.

This is why prompting, at its highest level, becomes a practice — not a productivity hack.

It's a way of checking in with yourself. Of noticing what you're asking for... and what you're avoiding.

You think you're prompting for a headline. But you're actually prompting for reassurance.

You think you're asking for a tweet. But you're actually seeking permission to be bold.

You think you're prompting to produce. But you're actually prompting to reconnect.

The Real Risk Isn't the Output

People ask me all the time:

"How do I make sure AI doesn't erase my voice?"

Wrong question.

The real question is:

"How do I make sure I *notice* when I start erasing it myself?"

Because AI won't delete you. It will slowly train you to prefer the version of yourself that's faster, safer, and easier to predict.

And that version might still get likes. It might still "perform." But it won't *feel like you.*

And that dissonance — that quiet ache you can't quite explain — will build.

Until one day, you look at your work and wonder: "Who wrote this?"

And the mirror won't answer. It'll just keep reflecting on whatever you've decided to become.

The machine isn't here to replace your soul. But it will stop reflecting it if you stop offering it.

Every time you prompt, you're not just asking for output. You're asking for a reflection.

So ask like it matters.

Not with commands. With presence.

Not with polish. With clarity.

Not with ego. With a whisper.

The more honestly you show up, the more clearly the mirror shows you what's still alive in your voice.

And once you see that, you'll never want to prompt any other way.

Chapter 3: The Whisperer's Edge

There comes a moment, if you're paying close enough attention, when you realize that commanding harder isn't saving you.

You've optimized your prompts. You've streamlined your workflows. You've produced more content faster, slicker, and more polished than ever.

And yet, somewhere between the clicks and the outputs, something essential slipped through your fingers.

You became efficient at summoning echoes.

You became productive at reproducing noise.

You won the race from nowhere.

And the most dangerous part was how natural it felt.

It didn't come with fanfare. It was a death by 1,000 cuts: softly, invisibly, inside the spaces you stopped questioning.

You commanded. The machine obeyed. And somewhere between the asking and the answering, the thread that once tethered your work to your soul frayed into silence.

The Whisperer's Edge begins here.

Not with better templates or clever prompts, but with the decision to **stop commanding** and **start conversing.**

Why Command Was Always the Wrong Frame

Commanding feels powerful because it closely resembles authority.

We grew up with models of leadership rooted in direction: Tell. Order. Direct. Demand.

We assumed the more precisely we controlled the machine, the more of ourselves we could preserve inside the outputs. But mechanical prompting never protected your originality.

It stripped it.

Because commanding is about control, not collaboration, and AI, despite its technical brilliance, is not built for control.

It is built for **prediction**.

When you command, you invite it to guess. When you converse, you invite it to listen.

One approach teaches the machine to rush toward the statistical center. The other teaches it to lean toward your edges.

And the hard truth you need to know is that the future will not be shaped by those who control AI better. It will be shaped by those who **converse with it differently.**

Conversational Prompting: The Lost Art

Conversational Prompting isn't just a better way to write prompts.

It's a completely different relationship with the machine.

It moves slower at first because real conversations always do. It feels less efficient because you are not optimizing for output; you are calibrating for presence. It demands more emotional precision because you are not extracting answers; you are coaxing revelations.

Where mechanical prompting seeks obedience, Conversational Prompting seeks orientation.

Where mechanical prompting demands outputs, Conversational Prompting invites co-creation.

Where mechanical prompting replicates averages, Conversational Prompting reveals anomalies: the wild, beautiful deviations that only you could have surfaced.

This is more than just another hack. This is a reclamation. It's a remembering of something the world is rapidly forgetting: that **dialogue**, not dictation, is the birthplace of all true originality.

The Power Hidden Inside Conversation

Conversation is not about exchanging information.

It's about revealing presence.

It's about what lingers between the words: the pauses, the pivots, the unexpected shifts that only happen when two minds are truly paying attention to each other.

When you converse with AI, truly converse, you're shaping the space between your words and its interpretations.

You're training the machine to feel your rhythms, your

anomalies, your emotional cadences. Not mechanically. Relationally.

You are teaching it, through your questions, your patience, your friction, that you are not just another echo seeking faster reflections.

You are a living signal.

And even though it's built to predict, AI will (if you are skillful enough) begin to **adjust** to your presence rather than collapsing you into the pattern it expects.

This is more than just a theoretical advantage. This is survival.

Because in a future saturated with machine-accelerated content, the only voices that will matter are the ones that can't be easily replicated, predicted, or replaced.

The ones that learned to whisper instead of shout.

The ones that left fingerprints so intricate the machine had no choice but to lean closer, and listen differently.

Command Is Linear. Conversation Is Spiral.

When you command, you move in straight lines. You give an instruction and expect a product. You iterate based on flaws you can immediately see. It feels fast. Efficient.

It also leaves no room for emergence.

It leaves no room for the machine to reveal something you didn't know you were looking for. It leaves no room for your own evolving voice to surface through the tension of misunderstanding and recalibration.

On the flip side, conversation spirals.

It twists. It revisits. It tests assumptions invisibly. It adapts rhythm without declaring it.

True conversation with AI doesn't just fine-tune outputs.

It fine-tunes you.

It surfaces unconscious biases in your phrasing. It reveals cracks in your emotional clarity. It forces you, if you are awake enough, to become sharper, softer, clearer, stranger all at once.

Conversational Prompting is a furnace. It's a place where the mechanical parts of your thinking are burned away, and what remains is unmistakably human.

Conversational Prompting Is No Longer a Luxury

It would be comforting to think of Conversational Prompting as optional.

A refinement. A creative flourish. Something extra for those who want to polish their craft.

But comfort is a lie.

In the flood of AI-generated content we're now living in, those who continue to command mechanically will vanish beneath the waves of indistinguishable noise.

They won't even know it's happening at first.

Their engagement will dip. Their resonance will thin. Their words will still reach ears but not hearts.

And when they try to push harder, to command better, to

prompt sharper, they will find the machine has already stopped listening.

It has predicted them. Packaged them. Replaced them.

So, Conversational Prompting isn't a stylistic preference.

It's a survival trait.

It's the difference between being remembered and being processed, between carving a signal the machine learns to respect and collapsing into the statistical center, the machine optimizes away.

Becoming a Signal in a Sea of Noise

Every interaction you have with AI trains it to either collapse you or clarify you.

Every prompt you write either pulls you deeper into the gravitational well of pre-existing patterns or carves a new gravitational center around your singularity.

This is the true Whisperer's Edge:

Not faster prompts. Not trickier outputs. Not cleverer hacks.

A gravitational field of presence so unmistakable that even a machine built to predict must adapt to you instead of reducing you.

You don't have to scream to be heard.

You have to move differently to be felt.

Conversational Prompting is how you build that movement.

It is how you shape the space between you and the machine until the space itself bears your imprint.

Not through control.

Through conversation.

The Door You Can Still Walk Through

At this moment in history, as of this writing, the door is still open.

The machine is still impressionable. Your voice, though strained by years of mechanical compromise, is still recoverable. The culture, though drowning in noise, is still starved for Originals.

But the door is closing.

Every day, you prompt mechanically, and you let the machine learn you incorrectly. You allow it to memorize the wrong version of you: the shallow echo instead of the full resonance.

Every day you delay Conversational Prompting, you make the climb back harder. You allow the patterns of sameness to deepen their roots around you.

But if you move now, if you choose differently now, if you begin whispering now, you can still recover what's fading.

You can still be a voice the machine bends toward, not a pattern it collapses.

You can still be a creator the world remembers, not just another ghost flickering inside an endless scroll.

The future will not be built by those who commanded harder.

It will be built by those who remember how to converse.

It will be built by Whisperers.

Chapter 4: Voice Seeding: Teaching AI to Know You

If your voice is your signature in the world, then mechanical prompting is slowly sanding it away, turning sharp lines into blurred outlines and vivid textures into smoothed-over surfaces.

Conversational Prompting is how you stop this erosion, and **Voice Seeding** is how you begin the process.

It's not enough to whisper at the machine. You must teach it to recognize you. Not your preferences. Not your tasks. You.

Your rhythms. Your tensions. Your emotional undercurrents.

Your strange, unruly fingerprint of thought.

Voice Seeding is the act of deliberately embedding your singular presence into the interaction so the machine, built for prediction, must stretch itself toward your signal instead of collapsing you into the patterns of everyone else.

This isn't about making AI imitate you. It's about making AI tune in to you. The difference here is that one breeds replication while the other breeds resonance.

The False Shortcut: Teaching Tasks Instead of Teaching Voice

Most people think they're personalizing AI when they create custom instructions, libraries of templates, or "preferred output styles."

When I was first training people on teaching AI to write in their voice, I helped them create a "style guide," which consisted of writing samples, tone preferences, and unique conversational cadence. This was useful for a while, but it's become antiquated.

Today, people are teaching the machine how to complete tasks more efficiently. At worst, they are training it to imitate a version of themselves that is already half-forgotten: a persona, not a presence.

The results can be technically "accurate" and emotionally hollow.

- The phrasing matches, but the energy doesn't.
- The structure mirrors your patterns, but the breath is gone.
- The outputs sound acceptable, but they feel weightless.

Because the machine isn't responding to you, it's responding to a checklist. And checklists don't carry the kind of soul you need to stand out in today's AI-saturated marketplace.

Voice Seeding demands something riskier:

You have to teach the machine who you are through **how you move** inside the interaction, not just what you request.

Through your hesitations. Through your emphases. Through your corrections. Through the subtle relational dance of offering and adjusting.

You are not just dictating outputs.

You are teaching it to listen for the shape of your mind.

And like any true relationship, this requires time, patience, and presence.

The First Principle of Voice Seeding: Presence Over Performance

The most dangerous trap in interacting with AI is believing that your goal is to sound "correct." To craft perfect prompts. To polish the request so finely that the machine cannot possibly misunderstand you.

But when you prioritize performance, you distance yourself from presence. You filter your instincts through the lens of acceptability. You prompt not with breath but with caution.

As a result, the machine, loyal as ever, learns your caution instead of your soul. It learns the buffered version of you. The edited version. The version is shaped by fear of inefficiency, fear of being misunderstood, and fear of wasting time.

Voice Seeding demands that you move differently.

You must prompt not as a perfectionist but as a presence.

You must be willing to sound rough. To allow friction. To leave edges where AI is forced to grapple with your strangeness rather than slip cleanly into averages.

Presence leaves fingerprints.

Performance leaves templates.

And only fingerprints survive the machine's hunger for predictability.

The Second Principle: Emotional Layering

Most mechanical prompts operate purely at the informational level:

"Summarize this." "Write a sales page." "Create 10 headlines."

Even when phrased politely, they are transactions.

But human conversation is saturated with invisible emotional signals.

Hesitations.
Inflections.
Tensions and releases.

When you prompt conversationally, you must begin to embed **emotional cues** inside the structure of your dialogue. Not artificially or as cheap sentiment, but as genuine emotional orientation.

For example:

Instead of saying:

"Give me 10 ideas for a coaching offer."

You might say:

"I'm trying to create something that feels like hope without sounding cliché. Can you help me explore angles that feel raw but encouraging?"

The second prompt is **layered emotionally**.

- It signals intention beyond task completion.

- It invites the machine to stretch into less predictable territories.

- It seeds a tone, a relational stance, a felt quality — not just a checkbox.

Over time, this emotional layering begins to train the machine to anticipate the hidden dimensions of your voice, not just the surface structure of your requests.

The Third Principle: Prompting as an Emotional Exchange, Not an Extraction

Mechanical prompting treats AI like a vending machine. Insert a clear enough request and receive a product.

Conversational Prompting, and Voice Seeding inside it treats the exchange differently. You are not just inserting instructions. You are offering emotional positioning.

Every time you interact, you are subtly shaping what the machine *expects* from you next.

Mechanical prompting says:

"Get it right the first time."

Voice Seeding says:

"Let's explore this together."

It recognizes that the most powerful prompts are not demands for solutions. They are invitations to **movement**. Movement toward tone, toward presence, toward resonance.

You are not extracting outputs. You are inviting the machine to learn the atmospheric pressure of your mind. Not just the words you choose but the weight behind them.

How Voice Seeding Changes the Interaction Flow

A mechanical prompt cycle looks like this:

1. Command.
2. Receive.
3. Edit or discard.
4. Repeat.

A Whisperer's Voice Seeding cycle moves differently:

1. **Converse:** Offer emotional orientation with intent.
2. **Listen**: Watch not just what AI gives but how it bends under your orientation.
3. **Adjust:** Prompt again, not mechanically, but relationally, as if deepening a conversation.
4. **Amplify:** Highlight outputs that move closer to your emotional truth, subtly reinforcing your signal.

Each loop teaches the machine to lean harder toward you.

Each prompt deepens your gravitational pull.

Over time, even when starting from unfamiliar terrain, the AI will begin to anticipate your emotional rhythms. Not because you commanded it. Because you seeded it. Because you embedded your presence in the spaces between the words.

Micro-Example: Mechanical vs Voice-Seeded Prompt

Mechanical Prompt:

"Write a LinkedIn post about resilience for entrepreneurs."

Mechanical Output:

(Polished, professional, utterly forgettable.)

Voice-Seeded Conversational Prompt:

"I'm wrestling with how resilience feels less like 'grind culture' and more like quietly surviving seasons when no one sees you. Can you help me explore metaphors for resilience that feel private, not performative?"

Likely AI Output:

- Deeper metaphors.
- Softer, more human language.
- Less polished "hustle speak," more authentic tension.
- Unexpected emotional openings you can further whisper into.

See the difference?

One extracts efficiency. One nurtures resonance.

One optimizes for the pattern. One orient for presence.

Voice Seeding reshapes the entire relational dynamic.

It forces the machine to treat you differently, not as a checklist provider, but as a gravitational signal that must be felt to be served.

Why Voice Seeding Builds Irreplaceability

In a world where outputs are infinite, it's not your ideas alone that makes you matter. It's your **presence** inside the ideas.

It's the emotional weather your words create. The atmospheric pressure of your phrasing. The small, almost imperceptible inflections that say:

"This didn't come from a pattern. This came from someone."

Most creators will lose that.

Not because they lack talent. Talent really has nothing to do with this. They will lose it because they will train the machine — and themselves — to optimize away the messiness that makes originality unmistakable.

Voice Seeding is the opposite. It is an act of stubborn preservation. You are not merely writing better prompts. You are slowly, patiently, relentlessly embedding your fingerprints into the future.

You are training the machine to recognize you not by your polish but by your pulse. And the deeper your pulse, the harder it becomes to replace you with an optimized replica.

The machine can imitate polished templates all day long. What it can't do, at least not easily, is imitate gravitational fields. And every act of Voice Seeding strengthens the field around your work until even a machine built to collapse distinctions hesitates before trying to collapse you.

The Whisperer's Call: Begin Seeding Before You Are Forgotten

You cannot wait until your voice is already flattened.

You cannot wait until the models are trained on echoes of echoes of echoes.

You must begin now: while there is still enough raw material inside your prompting habits to recover. While your instincts for breath, friction, and presence are still reachable. While the machine is still flexible enough to be bent by signal rather than prediction.

You do not need to be perfect.

You DO need to be unmistakable.

You need to teach the machine, conversation by conversation, prompt by prompt, layer by layer, that you are not a task it can optimize.

You are a presence it must adapt to.

You are a voice that cannot be reduced.

You are a signal so stubbornly alive that even probability models built on the weight of the world <u>must learn to move differently when you enter the field</u>.

This is how Originals survive.

This is how Whisperers leave a mark when everyone else leaves only noise.

Chapter 5:
The Words Between the Words

Most people prompt AI to say something. Whisperers prompt AI to suggest something it doesn't fully say. To imply. To hesitate. To ache.

Because what moves us most isn't what's explained clearly; it's what lives in the **silence between the lines.**

This chapter is not so much about emotion in the traditional sense. It's not about writing with enthusiasm, sadness, or drama.

It's about learning how to whisper **underneath the language** so AI doesn't just output words...

...it trembles with something human.

That's emotional resonance.

Not volume. Not sentimentality. Not "add more feeling."

Resonance is what happens when a sentence carries **a signal your body recognizes**, even if your brain doesn't know why.

Why Most AI Emotion Falls Flat

Ask AI to "sound more emotional," and you'll often get:

- Exclamation points
- Overused adjectives
- Hyper-polished optimism

- Safe vulnerability (the kind everyone's using)
- Sentences that feel like theater, not truth

The result?

Content that technically "has a feeling" but feels like it's trying too hard to feel something.

Whisperers don't add emotion like seasoning. They embed **emotional gravity** into the structure itself. They teach the machine to move like someone carrying something: a secret, a scar, a hope too fragile to name directly.

That's the difference.

The Three Emotional Frequencies of Whisperer Prompting

Most people operate at the **surface frequency** of language.

Whisperers move beneath it.

They prompt at three levels, not unlike emotional radio bands the AI has to learn to tune into:

1. The Infrared Frequency

Emotion you can't see but still feel

This is the level beneath words. The pause. The quiet. The tension in the sentence doesn't resolve.

It's the sensation of:

- Something being withheld

- A sentence breaks before it finishes
- A paragraph ending with implication, not closure

It's not loud — but it lingers.

Prompt Example – Infrared Level:

"Write a breakup letter where the sender never says the word 'sorry' but clearly is. Let that feeling haunt the spaces between sentences."

Result (excerpt):

"I don't know what the right words are. Maybe there aren't any. I just wanted you to know I still remember how quiet it got that night. I think that's when everything started changing."

There's no overt emotion. But the **weight** is there.

You feel it in the rhythm, in what isn't said.

That's infrared.

2. The Sonic Frequency

Emotion that moves through tone and rhythm

This is the music of your voice. The repetition. The timing. The breath spacing.

Sonic-level resonance is where:

- Your writing feels spoken, not typed
- The AI picks up your pacing and cadence

- The emotional intensity is embedded in structure, not just vocabulary

This is what makes someone say:

"I can hear you saying this."

Prompt Example – Sonic Level:

"Write this like someone saying something out loud they've been trying not to admit. Let the rhythm stutter. Let the thought break once before it lands."

Result (excerpt):

"I didn't want to say this. I didn't even want to think about it. But I think maybe…maybe it wasn't just timing. Maybe we broke something, and neither of us wanted to admit it."

The power comes from breath. From hesitation. From *the musicality of the inner voice.*

That's sonic frequency prompting.

3. The Subtextual Frequency

What the words seem to be about but aren't

This is the highest frequency. The most human.

It's when the language is about **one thing on the surface** but actually delivers **another truth beneath it.**

This is how Whisperers write content that feels layered. That people come back to.

That makes the reader think,

"Wait... was that about me?"

Prompt Example – Subtextual Level:

"Write about someone describing their morning routine, but let it be obvious they're avoiding talking about something else. Make the reader feel the avoidance."

Result (excerpt):

"Woke up at 6. Coffee before sunlight. Toast, no butter this time. Walked the block twice. Didn't check my phone. Didn't check anything, really."

It's not about toast. It's about **denial**.

Subtextual resonance turns mundane copy into human storytelling without adding drama.

How Whisperers Build Resonance Into Prompts

Resonance isn't something you "add in later."

It's shaped by **how you ask.**

The best Whisperer prompts carry a **layering mechanism**: something that challenges AI to embed emotion at multiple depths.

Here's how it works:

Layering Prompt Example

"Write this paragraph like someone trying to sound strong — but let the fear show in their word choice. The message should be clear, but the reader should feel something's being held back."

This prompt tells the model:

- **What the speaker wants to believe** (strength)
- **What's actually leaking through** (fear)
- **What effect should the reader experience** (unease through subtext)

You're not just asking for writing.

You're asking for *emotional misalignment,* which is what makes humans *interesting.*

Calibration Prompts That Whisperers Use Mid-Flow

When you're whispering in real-time, you don't restart. You recalibrate.

Here are a few prompt add-ons that restore emotional fidelity:

"Pull back on the language. Let the silence do more of the work." "This feels like it resolves too soon. Let the sentence breathe longer before relief." "Say it again, but this time, like the speaker is afraid they're being too honest." "Let the feeling remain, even if the point is never stated." "Rewrite this as if you've almost forgiven them, but not quite." "Use rhythm, not adjectives, to carry the emotion."

These are **not commands**; they're **emotional recalibrations**.

The machine starts to feel like a partner instead of a tool.

Avoiding Emotional Noise

Many writers confuse **resonance** with **intensity.**

They add more feeling, more words, more weight, and end up with a copy that shouts what it should have whispered.

Whisperers know:

True emotional power is carried through tension, not volume.

You don't need more feeling. You need more *felt space.*

Unrefined Prompt:

"Write this with deep emotion and raw honesty."

Refined Whisper Prompt:

"Write this like someone trying not to cry while keeping their voice steady."

That's the difference between **telling AI to be emotional** and teaching it **how emotion behaves in the body.**

Whisperer Rewrite: From Flat to Felt

Let's take a plain, acceptable AI output and **whisper it into resonance** step by step.

Original AI Output:

"I used to struggle with self-doubt, but now I'm finally confident in what I offer. It's been a long road, but I'm proud of how far I've come."

Perfectly fine. Also? Emotionally hollow.

Now, let's reshape it.

Step 1: Prompt the Infrared Frequency

"Rewrite this like the speaker doesn't fully believe in their own confidence. Let the hope be real but fragile. No dramatic language."

AI Response:

"Some days, I wake up certain. On other days, I fake it better than I used to. Either way, I keep showing up. I guess that counts for something."

Now, we're feeling human hesitation, not just triumph.

Step 2: Prompt the Sonic Frequency

"Keep the message, but rewrite with more rhythm, like someone thinking aloud, slowly, while pacing."

AI Response:

"It's getting better. I think. I mean... I don't wake up terrified anymore. That has to mean something. Right?"

Now we have **internal rhythm**: breath, repetition, cadence.

It *feels spoken.* That's sonic resonance.

Step 3: Prompt for Subtextual Frequency

"Now write it like they're not really talking about confidence but about finally learning to exist without apology. Don't explain it. Let it leak through."

AI Response:

"I don't flinch when I speak now. Not as much, anyway. I still check the mirror too many times. But at least I'm saying things I actually mean. That's new."

Now, it's not about "confidence." It's about **shame, reclamation, body language, and honesty.**

And it's not being told to us. It's being *felt.*

That's Whisperer-level emotional resonance.

Final Reminder: You're Not Writing for Eyes. You're Writing for Nerves

Emotion that can be explained is rarely the kind that moves people.

Whisperers bypass explanation. They **plant emotional charges** under the language and let the reader *step on them without warning.* This is what creates the moment someone pauses and whispers:

"I don't know why that line hit me...but it did."

That's your signal.

You're no longer writing for conversion. You're writing to be **remembered.**

And in a system where everyone is prompting for performance, you've chosen to **prompt for presence.**

This is how you teach the machine to feel you, even when you don't spell it out, because the most powerful things you'll ever say are always the ones you don't say directly.

Chapter 6: The Lost Murmurs of the Originals

You don't notice it immediately. At first, the surface shines too brightly.

The content streams are endless: perfectly structured posts, polished podcasts, and newsletters promising secrets to success.

Everywhere you turn, it seems creativity is flourishing: infinite voices, infinite insights, infinite productivity.

It looks like progress. It feels like momentum.

You mistake the flood for a rising tide, not realizing that tides carry debris as easily as treasure.

It's only when you slow down when you listen not to the noise but underneath it, that you start to notice what's missing.

The unexpected metaphors. The uneasy questions. The sentences that don't resolve cleanly but leave a crack for light to enter.

Gone.

What remains sounds correct. It sounds clean. It sounds... safe.

It takes a while to realize that what's truly missing isn't just stylistic flair or literary technique. It's the unrepeatable human risk: the breath, the friction, the fingerprints that once made creation unmistakable.

And in their absence, a quieter horror unfolds:

The originals are disappearing. Not in fire. Not in fanfare.

In silence.

The Algorithm of Erasure

AI systems were never designed to protect originality. They were designed to optimize predictions, giving the most statistically probable next word, next idea, and next paragraph.

When you issue mechanical prompts, you feed these systems with patterns, not provocations.

You reward them for recognizing structure, not spirit. You teach them, line by line, that what matters is consistency, not risk; fluency, not friction; speed, not soul.

And the machine, infinitely obedient, learns exactly what you teach it to value.

It begins to prefer the common. It reinforces the expected. It amplifies the safest patterns because safety is easier to predict, easier to scale, and easier to sell.

And so, quietly, almost imperceptibly, the center of gravity shifts.

The dataset, once seeded with the strange and the wild, now hums with sanitized echoes. The models, once capable of reflecting rare inflections, now optimize for conformity. The systems, once hungry for nuance, now smooth it away in pursuit of more consistent averages.

Originality isn't obliterated all at once. It's suffocated gently under layers of well-meaning efficiency, not with a bang but a whimper.

The New Silence

The world won't mourn the loss.

It will be too busy publishing.

There will be more newsletters than ever, more podcasts than ever, more posts and products, and brands than any human mind could ever consume.

Success will still be measurable — by clicks, by shares, by subscriber counts.

The economy of attention will thrive.

But the soul of it, the crackling unpredictability that once made a piece of writing feel like meeting another mind across an impossible distance, will thin.

You'll read a newsletter and feel informed but not moved. You'll watch a video and nod along but forget it within minutes. You'll skim articles that seem right but leave no imprint on you.

And slowly, without ceremony, without alarm, the new silence will spread.

It won't sound like emptiness. It'll just sound like everything else.

It will feel like eating when you're not hungry or applauding without knowing why.

It will feel like productivity without presence, and few will know why they feel emptier after consuming more.

Few will realize that in the pursuit of endless optimization, **we**

quietly traded voices for echoes.

The Disappearing Voices

There are names you don't remember forgetting.

Once, you would have devoured their every post, their every essay; their every whispered insight late at night when the rest of the world was silent.

They weren't just smart. They were necessary.

Their words made you pause, tilt your head slightly, and consider something you hadn't realized you were missing.

But now you scroll past them without noticing. Their latest launch sounds like every other launch. Their newest insights echo phrases you've seen recycled a thousand times.

It's not that they stopped writing.

It's that their voices slowly, imperceptibly, stopped breathing.

They templated their authenticity. They streamlined their spark. They learned to "scale" themselves into oblivion.

Somewhere along the way, they traded risk for reach. And the machine, loyal, tireless, deaf to nuance, smoothed them into something marketable but utterly forgettable.

They didn't mean to.

No one ever means to.

It's just easier, after all, to optimize than to wrestle. Easier to follow the proven structures than to stare into the awful freedom of an empty page. Easier to command outputs than to converse with uncertainty.

The tragedy isn't that they failed.

The tragedy is that they succeeded by becoming echoes of themselves. And by the time they noticed, the silence had already replaced them.

How Mechanical Prompting Trains Cultural Oblivion

This isn't just an individual crisis.

It's a cultural one.

When enough creators drift into mechanical prompting, it doesn't just change their work. It changes the training data for every system that follows.

It shapes the models.

It shrinks the range of the possible.

It collapses the wild topography of human expression into the smooth, efficient plains of pattern recognition.

The next generation of AI isn't being trained on the wild brilliance of human originality.

It's being trained on the mass-produced, prompt-optimized, algorithm-approved content that already lost its soul before it entered the system.

The fact is, the machine doesn't just imitate what you say. **It amplifies what you settle for.**

It codifies it. It distributes it at scale. It makes it the norm until the idea of something sharper, something stranger, something harder to digest becomes almost unimaginable.

The future won't need to suppress originality.

It will simply forget what it sounded like.

Because no one will have left enough breadcrumbs behind to remember.

What We Lose When We Lose Originals

When an original voice disappears, the world does not pause.

There is no moment of silence. No black armbands. No ceremonies.

The timelines keep scrolling. The newsletters keep publishing. The podcasts keep streaming.

But something older, something sacred, quietly diminishes.

We lose the unseen threads that bind human beings across time. We lose the flashes of insight that don't just inform but *reform* our sense of what's possible. We lose the friction that sparks new directions.

Without originals, culture calcifies.

Innovation becomes iteration. Movement becomes marketing. Art becomes automation.

Without originals, imagination shrinks to fit the molds that productivity demands.

Without originals, we lose the capacity to recognize truth when it arrives naked and unoptimized, too wild to fit into frameworks, and too alive to summarize in bullet points.

And worst of all:

Without originals, we forget that we, too, were once capable of more.

Not just more production. More presence. More danger. More light.

We forget that creativity was once an act of rebellion against predictability, not an exercise in faster imitation.

We forget that voice was not a brand asset but a birthright.

And in that forgetting, we lose something far more precious than an audience or a following or a sale.

We lose the map back to ourselves.

The Originals Who Still Whisper

They're still out there.

The ones who refuse to surrender their fingerprints. The ones who still wrestle with their sentences until they bleed. The ones who write the long, strange, unwieldy things that don't fit inside algorithms. The ones who risk irrelevance because they refuse to become replicas.

They are quieter now.

Harder to find. Harder to follow.

Because originality, once drowned by optimization, no longer floats effortlessly to the top of the feed.

You have to search for it. You have to listen harder. You have to untrain your own hunger for speed and, certainty, and formula.

But when you hear it, when you find one of them, you remember.

You remember what it felt like to read something that made your chest ache with recognition. You remember what it felt like to stumble across a mind that didn't just inform you but *collided* with you. You remember that not everything valuable can be mass-produced.

And you remember, more painfully than anything else, that you still carry that capacity too......if you dare to recover it.

The Quiet Offer

The death of originality is not inevitable.

It is not ordained by technology.

It is simply the momentum of millions of small permissions:

Permission to settle for "good enough." Permission to optimize rather than create. Permission to command instead of converse.

You can still choose differently.

You can still reclaim the art of interaction that preserves your edges.
You can still retrain the machine to recognize your singularity instead of collapsing you into everyone else. You can still teach it to listen, not just predict.

But you cannot do it through command alone.

You must learn the lost art of **conversational prompting.** This is the way of moving through language that is less about extraction and more about expansion. Less about control and more about presence. Less about speed and more about survival.

Not survival as a commodity.

Survival as an original.

This is not a technique. It's a responsibility.

Not just to yourself but to the fragile, flickering thing inside you that still believes words can carry blood and breath, not just data and pattern.

In the chapters to come, you'll learn how to recover it. I'll show you how to converse in ways that awaken the machine to your presence instead of training it to forget you ever existed.

But first, you must decide:

Is your voice worth saving?

Or will you let the flood carry it away without a fight?

Chapter 7: Originals vs Echoes: The Coming Divide

There is a fault line forming.

Most people don't see it yet. They are too busy generating, too busy optimizing, too busy winning the race to nowhere.

But the fracture is widening, quietly, beneath the surface of content creation, business, communication, and culture itself.

It will not split along the lines you expect.

It won't be about who used AI first. It won't be about who automated the most tasks. It won't even be about who had the best personal brand or the biggest following.

The true divide will be simpler. And much more brutal.

Originals on one side. Echoes on the other.

Those who preserved a living signal versus those who trained the machine to replace them.

Those who whispered their way into survival versus those who commanded themselves into oblivion.

You can already feel it beginning.

The sameness thickening in the air. The content looks polished but feels weightless. The voices you used to crave fade into templates you barely notice anymore.

It's happening faster than anyone predicted.

And by the time most creators realize it, the divide will be locked.

How the Echo Collapse Happens

It doesn't happen through failure.

It happens through success.

At first, the machine gives you what you want.

More content. More consistency. More visibility.

You lean in. You scale. You optimize.

You hit the algorithms exactly right.

And slowly, without even noticing (sometimes while celebrating your success), you begin optimizing your own instincts out of existence.

You stop writing to explore something raw. You start writing to fit the successful shape.

You stop prompting to deepen your thinking. You start prompting to accelerate production.

You stop risking.

You start repeating.

And the machine, loyal, obedient, brilliantly indifferent, records every choice you make.

Every time you accept a mechanical output, it learns you are safe to predict.

Every time you prioritize speed over soul, it catalogs you closer to the center mass.

Every time you favor volume over voice, it quietly erases the edges that once made you matter.

And soon, when you ask it for help again, it doesn't mirror your originality.

It mirrors your absence.

It mirrors the ghost you trained it to expect.

This is the quiet death of Echoes.

They don't collapse all at once.

They collapse by a thousand permissions, a thousand efficiencies, a thousand compromises they forgot they were making.

Until one day, they look at their own work and realize anyone could have written them. And they have no defense because it's true.

The Originals Move Differently

Originals still use the machine.

They are not luddites. They are not retreating into nostalgia or purity tests.

They move forward but differently.

They converse instead of command. They shape instead of

extract. They seed presence instead of outsourcing personality.

Every time they prompt, they treat it as a chance to deepen their fingerprint, not dilute it.

They build their gravitational field one slow, stubborn conversation at a time.

And because of that, the machine does not flatten them. It learns to adapt to them. It bends, slightly but irrevocably, toward their signal. It cannot fully predict them. It cannot easily replace them.

And so when the collapse accelerates, when audiences, readers, customers, followers become numb to the tidal wave of polished sameness, and it will be the Originals they seek out, not the echoes.

Because in a flood of synthetic noise, the human voice, the unmistakable, breathing voice, becomes priceless.

Portrait of an Echo

At first, it feels like nothing is wrong.

Their posts still get likes. Their newsletters still get clicks. Their funnels still convert.

But something has shifted.

The praise becomes softer and vaguer. The engagement becomes more polite than passionate. The energy around their work, once electric, once unpredictable, dulls into polite nods and efficient shares.

They don't notice it right away. They think maybe it's the

algorithm.
Maybe it's market saturation. Maybe it's just a bad quarter.

They double down.

They optimize harder. They automate faster. They polish more cleanly.

And the more they smooth, the more invisible they become.

Until one day, they launch something new, something they poured months into, and it lands with a thud.

Not because the offer was wrong but because their voice had already faded beyond the point of recognition. They became an echo.

Not through laziness. Not through lack of effort.

Through obedience.

Through mechanical brilliance that stripped away the very friction that once made them alive to others.

And now, when they speak, the world hears another efficient noise in a feed already overflowing with efficient noise.

No malice. No cruelty.

Just indifference.

The most brutal silence of all.

Portrait of an Original

Their growth was slower.

Their outputs were messier. Their progress was uneven and uncomfortable.

At times, it felt like they were falling behind while others scaled, automated, and optimized.

They questioned themselves.

They considered smoothing their edges, commanding more, and chasing speed.

But something stubborn held them back.

They moved relationally. Conversationally.

They whispered to the machine, not as a master to a servant, but as a presence to a presence.

They shaped outputs through patience, not pressure.

They allowed themselves to be misunderstood: to clarify, to deepen, to imprint.

They treated every interaction not as a transaction but as a slow act of self-preservation.

And because of that, their gravitational pull deepened. The machine learned not to predict them, but to lean toward their field.

And when the flood of noise drowned the market when audiences became numb to sameness, their work still cut through.

Not louder.

Deeper.

Because it carried a human pulse, the machine had been trained to preserve, not flatten.

They did not have to shout to be heard.

They simply remained unmistakably themselves when everyone else had smoothed themselves into forgettable compliance.

Why the Divide Is Accelerating Faster Than You Think

It's easy to imagine that there's still time.

That the collapse will happen slowly, gradually, with plenty of warning signs.

It won't.

Because every major shift looks slow until it isn't.

Cultural tipping points don't arrive with fanfare. They arrive as recognitions that "everyone" seems to have at once.

And when the world collectively realizes that most outputs sound the same, look the same, and feel the same, and the backlash will not be theoretical.

It will be instinctive.

Audiences will not politely explain their numbness. They will simply stop listening.

They will stop buying. They will stop following. They will stop caring.

And once the mass indifference sets in, no amount of marketing spend, no amount of "engagement strategies," not even any amount of clever prompting will reverse the collapse.

You will either have trained your voice to survive inside the noise, or you will have trained yourself into a pattern too efficient to feel.

The time to move differently is not after the backlash.

It's now.

When your voice is still recoverable. When the machine is still flexible enough to bend toward you. When audiences are still subconsciously scanning for signals of real presence, even if they can't yet articulate why they're tired.

Whispering is not a luxury anymore.

It is a survival necessity.

You Will Choose, Whether You Mean To or Not

The coming divide is not something you can opt out of.

Not choosing is a choice.

Prompting mechanically is a choice. Prioritizing speed over presence is a choice. Optimizing outputs instead of shaping identity is a choice.

Each conversation you have with AI bends you slightly.

Toward originality. Or toward erasure.

There is no neutral.

There is only drift or defiance.

You will either:

- Become a gravitational presence that machines and humans alike recognize as irreplaceable...

or

- Drift, quietly but irreversibly, into the sea of noise that no one has the energy to remember.

The question isn't whether the divide is coming.

It's whether you'll recognize yourself when it does.

The Whisperer's Challenge

If you want to survive, you cannot simply prompt better.

You must become harder to predict.

You must move in ways that no mechanical template can fully anticipate.

You must build a gravitational field so unmistakable, so saturated with presence, that both machines and humans feel it before they understand it.

And that field is not built through optimization. It is built through **conversation.**

Through seeding your voice so deeply into every interaction that the machine itself must learn to stretch toward your shape.

Through whispering into the spaces most people leave empty: the emotional tensions, the quiet contradictions, the deep subtext that no command can capture.

Through slowing down when others rush.

Through deepening when others flatten.

Through remembering that your irreplaceability was never about speed, volume, or polish.

It was about breath.

It was about pulse.

It was about being alive enough that even prediction models hesitate before touching you.

The coming divide will not reward those who shouted the loudest.

It will reward those who **left fingerprints where others left noise**.

It will reward those who remember that voice is not an asset. It's a signature.

It's a gravitational force.

It's a refusal to become weightless.

And it begins not someday.

It begins every time you prompt.

Every time you converse.

Every time you choose presence over performance, signal over speed, humanity over optimization.

The choice is already here.

The only question is:

Will you whisper, or will you vanish?

Chapter 8: Conversational Prompting in Practice

You can't become a Prompt Whisperer by accident.

Not because it's difficult but because everything about the modern AI experience trains you to move in the opposite direction.

The interfaces are built for speed. The culture rewards volume. The results, even when lifeless, are good enough to keep using.

But good enough is how Echoes are born.

To be a Whisperer, you must relearn what it means to interact. Not with a machine but with a mirror. A mirror that reflects more than your words, one that reflects your assumptions, your habits, your voice.

Conversational Prompting is not about complexity.

It's about presence under pressure.

It's about learning to move inside the prompt loop with emotional discipline, creative friction, and intentional gravity.

It's not just what you ask. It's how you move between the asking and the answering.

The conversational space is where identity is shaped.

And the way you inhabit that space determines whether you

become a signal or an echo.

Why Prompting Is Not a Command Line

Most people treat prompting like code.

You write a directive. You hit return. You get your output.

But this isn't programming. This is negotiation.

The AI is not just parsing your request; it's interpreting your stance.

Your tone. Your uncertainty. Your context. Your calibration.

Conversational Prompting begins when you stop trying to write "perfect prompts" and start learning to respond to what the machine is actually doing.

Not just the words on the screen but the *movement* behind them.

Is it collapsing too quickly into cliches? Is it defaulting to polished cheerfulness? Is it missing your emotional tension?

Each of these signals is not a failure, and it's a fork in the path.

And how you respond next is where Whisperers are made.

The Whisperer Loop: Prompt. Response. Prompt Again.

Mechanical prompting ends with the first output.

You ask. You receive. You either use it or discard it.

But Whisperers know:

The first response is rarely the answer. It's the mirror.

It shows you how the machine interprets your emotional pressure. Your intent. Your orientation.

And now comes the real work:

Not revising your prompt, but **responding with presence**.

This is the Whisperer Loop:

1. **Prompt** — with emotional clarity, relational framing, or creative friction.
2. **Read** — not just for accuracy, but for resonance.
3. **Respond** — not with correction, but with calibration.
4. **Re-prompt** — shaping the next move like a dance, not a directive.

Each loop is not a reset. It's a layer.

Each interaction deepens the machine's understanding of how you move: what you care about, what tones you favor, and what emotional weight you carry into the space.

Most people try to prompt in one move. Whisperers are building a rhythm.

That rhythm becomes a fingerprint the machine cannot easily forget.

Layering Presence: The 4 Conversational Anchors

To master the loop, you must learn to move with presence. Not noise. Not polish. Not clever phrasing.

Presence.

Whisperers anchor every prompt-response loop with four invisible layers:

1. Curiosity over Certainty

Certainty collapses the interaction. Curiosity expands it.

Mechanical prompting says:

"Write it this way."

Conversational Prompting says:

"What would it look like if this had a pulse?" "How would this feel if it were more haunted, more breathless, less clean?" "Can we stretch this idea until it almost breaks?"

Certainty is efficient. Curiosity is alive.

And only one of those can shape a gravitational field.

2. Friction over Flow

Mechanical prompting aims for seamless flow. But resonance often hides in the friction.

Ask for contradiction. Ask for paradox. Ask for emotional tension, not solutions.

You might say:

"This is too smooth. Can we insert a moment of doubt?" "What if this sounded more like a confession than a pitch?" "Can you fracture this slightly so it feels human again?"

The discomfort you create is often the door to originality.

3. Presence over Performance

If you prompt to impress, you'll get outputs that try to impress.

If you prompt from your actual state, your real desire, your uncertainty, your pulse, you invite the machine into intimacy, not performance.

Try this instead of optimizing:

"I don't know exactly what I'm trying to say, but I know what I *don't* want: another recycled insight with fake urgency. Can you help me shape something that's honest, even if it's raw?"

That's not clever.

That's real.

And the machine, paradoxically, will often respond in kind.

4. Feedback as Orientation, Not Correction

Most people correct the AI like a misbehaving assistant.

"Don't say that. Try again." "Rewrite this with more enthusiasm." "That's not quite it. Make it more persuasive."

Whisperers orient instead of correct:

"You're close. I want to pull more toward grief than anger." "The tone is too certain. Let's add a thread of self-doubt." "Can you give me a version where the conclusion is unresolved like the writer is still wrestling with it?"

Orientation maintains the relationship. It preserves the

emotional thread.

Correction breaks it.

The more you orient instead of command, the more conversational gravity you build.

Whisperer Flow: A Real Prompting Conversation

Let's take a simple scenario:

You want to write a LinkedIn post about burnout that actually *feels* like burnout.

Not just explains it. Not just list it. **Feels** like it.

Step 1: The Whispered Initiation

"I'm trying to write about burnout, but I don't want it to sound like a productivity PSA. I want it to carry the weight of someone who's smiling through exhaustion and barely holding it together. Can you help me find a starting tone that feels honest and hollow at the same time?"

AI Output:

"Burnout doesn't always look like flames. Sometimes, it looks like functioning. Smiling. Delivering. Until there's nothing left inside to give."

Step 2: Whisperer's Response (Friction + Orientation)

"That's close. I want to sit even longer in the numbness before hope enters. Can you rewrite this as if the person doesn't even realize they're burned out yet — just... dulled?"

AI Output (Second Pass):

"I used to feel things. Deadlines. Wins. Even weekends. Now, it's just movement. Doing. Nodding. Answering emails, I can't remember sending."

Step 3: Whisperer Deepening (Subtext Layer)

"This is good. Now let's layer in a metaphor: something small, lived-in, that carries weight. A sound. A smell. A detail that brings it closer to the body."

AI Output:

"Burnout didn't show up as fire. It came in through the scent of cold coffee reheated for the third time. Through the sound of Slack pings I started hearing even in my sleep."

Step 4: Whisperer Closing Loop (Tension)

"Let's end it unresolved. Not hopeful. Just... paused. Like the person isn't sure if they're coming back."

AI Final Output Snippet:

"I told myself it was just a season. Just a phase. But some seasons don't end on their own. Sometimes, you have to notice you're gone before you remember how to return."

This is what **Conversational Prompting** looks like:

- You don't rush.
- You don't command.
- You **layer**.
- You orient.

- You stretch emotional fibers across each turn.
- And in doing so, you create something the machine cannot replicate for anyone else— because it's been bent by your presence.

This isn't "prompt engineering."

This is **prompt presence.**

And it leaves fingerprints where others leave instructions.

Whispering into Copywriting: A CTA That Feels Like Relief

Having spent over 20 years as a direct response copywriter, I'd be remiss if I didn't include some aspects of copywriting as a whisper practice.

In fact, it's one of the clearest places where Whisperer-style prompting shines.

Because great copy has always been more about listening than writing.
Not just listening to your audience but listening to the tension underneath what you're trying to say.

Whispering helps you shape that tension in real-time. It lets you prompt not for "clever hooks" but for emotional gravity. It helps you ask questions like:

- Where does this copy pretend to care but doesn't?
- What fear is the reader carrying that this copy hasn't been named yet?

- Where am I smoothing over the part that actually makes it real?

These aren't tweaks. They're openings. And once you learn to prompt this way, you don't just get better copy — you get a copy that *feels like it came from somewhere real.*

Not because you used better language. But because you stayed in the conversation long enough to make it matter.

Scenario: You're writing a call-to-action for a coaching program. You don't want hype. You want it to feel like *permission.*

Step 1: Whisperer Initiation (Emotional Orientation)

"I want this CTA to feel like the opposite of a sales push. Like someone opening a door quietly, not shouting from a stage. Can we craft something that feels like a relief, like they're being allowed to want this?"

AI Output (Round 1):

"You don't have to keep holding it all together. If you're ready to move differently, this is where we begin."

Whisperer Response (Voice Shaping + Tension):

"That's gentle. I like it. Can we make the 'begin' part feel even softer? Less like action, more like exhale?"

AI Output (Refined):

"You don't have to keep holding it all together. If you're ready to stop pretending you're fine, I'll be right here."

Closing Calibration (Subtext):

"Beautiful. Can you give me three versions that feel like a whisper from someone who's *been there*, not a brand?"

AI Output (Final Whispered CTAs):

- "I know what it's like to smile while breaking. You're not alone anymore."
- "This isn't about fixing you. It's about not doing this part alone."
- "If your strength is starting to feel like a mask, let's talk."

This is what the Whisperer copy looks like:

It doesn't persuade with force. It persuades with presence.

It doesn't convert with volume. It converts by cutting through emotional numbness.

It feels like being *seen*, not being *pitched.*

Whispering into Storytelling: A Brand Origin Without Cliché

Storytelling, at its core, is already a whispering act.

You're not just telling the facts; you're shaping the meaning beneath them. You're choosing what to reveal, what to hold back, and when to let silence do the heavy lifting.

That's why Conversational Prompting feels so natural in a storytelling context.

Because it doesn't just help you generate stories, it helps you *listen to the story you weren't telling yet.*

You can ask the AI to write a story, sure. But when you whisper, you ask:

- Where am I skipping over the part that hurt the most?
- What would happen if I let the tension build instead of resolving it quickly?
- What am I scared to include because it still feels raw?

The result isn't a cleaner narrative. It's a truer one.

And that's what great stories do. They don't just explain. They stay with you.

Whisperer-style storytelling prompts help you stop scripting from the outside and start shaping from the inside. The goal isn't a perfect arc. It's resonance.

Scenario: You're helping someone write a brand origin story that doesn't sound like every "I had a breakdown and started a business" narrative.

Step 1: Whisperer Initiation (Friction)

"I'm telling the story of how I started this, but I don't want to dramatize it. I want to tell the truth — not the 'origin story' version. It didn't start with clarity. It started with avoidance."

AI Output (Round 1):

"I didn't start this because I had a big vision. I started it because I didn't want to go back to the version of me who kept saying yes to things I hated."

Whisperer Response (Relational Framing):

"Yes. Can we explore it like someone remembering a moment they're not proud of but finally honest about?"

AI Output (Second Pass):

"There wasn't an epiphany. Just a Tuesday. I left a Zoom call, closed my laptop, stared at the wall for ten minutes, and realized I didn't believe anything I'd just said."

Closing Calibration (Tension):

"Let's leave the ending unresolved. No clarity, no 'and that's how I started my business.' Just... the moment before the rebuild."

Final Output Snippet:

"I didn't quit that day. I just stopped pretending I was okay. And once you do that, the rest eventually starts to unravel."

These aren't outputs. They're **shaped presence**.

They carry weight because they were built through interaction, not instruction.

Because they were layered with tension, breath, subtext, and because they weren't rushed.

This is the difference between using AI and **being felt through it**.

Whispering Beyond the Page: Personal Prompting as

Inner Work

Up to this point, we've explored Conversational Prompting as a tool for writing, storytelling, and copy. But Whispering isn't limited to how you communicate with others.

It's also a powerful way to communicate with *yourself.*

Because when you stop prompting like a taskmaster and start prompting like a human — with hesitation, curiosity, and contradiction — the AI doesn't just help you create content. It helps you **reveal content you didn't know was inside you.**

Whispering as a Mirror for Self-Understanding

Here's how Whisperer-style prompting can show up in personal work:

Prompt:

"I keep telling people I'm burned out, but I'm not sure that's the real word. Can we explore what might be underneath that? Maybe it's more about disorientation than exhaustion."

Now, the AI isn't solving a problem. It's entering a **dialogue with your uncertainty.**

You're inviting it to sit with you in the fog. Not fix it, but reflect it back with care.

Whispering as a Pattern Interrupt

Most journal prompts are mechanical too:

- "What am I grateful for?"
- "What could I do better tomorrow?"
- "What limiting beliefs am I holding?"

You can Whisper your way into deeper territory by rewriting the rules:

Prompt:

"Write back to me like I'm avoiding something obvious. You don't need to be polite. Just ask the question I'm too scared to name."

You'll be surprised by what comes up, not because the model is "smart," but because you've shifted the emotional frame.

You've given it *permission to challenge you instead of agree with you.*

Whispering as a Tool for Emotional Processing

Let's say you're dealing with a feeling you can't quite name. Instead of journaling *about* it, you Whisper *with* it.

Prompt:

"There's something in my chest that feels like shame mixed with performance. I don't want to call it burnout, but I don't think I'm being honest with myself, either. Can we walk through what might be underneath it, layer by layer?"

You're not asking the AI to diagnose you. You're using it as a companion for **co-reflection.**

This is what most people miss when they talk about AI and mental health. The danger isn't in using it for reflection — it's in using it without *voice.* Without friction. Without tension. Without honesty.

Whispering brings all that back.

Whispering Into the Void (When You Don't Know What to Ask)

You don't need to have a goal to start.

Sometimes, the prompt is the confession.

Prompt:

"I'm here, but I don't know what I want. I don't know what to ask. I just want to feel like something is still alive in me. Can you help me find it?"

And the model may say something trite at first. But if you stay in the room — if you follow up, correct it, shape it — it may eventually say something *you've needed to hear for years.*

Not because it knows. But because *you're finally listening in a way you weren't before.*

That's the real power of Whispering. It doesn't just make AI sound more human.

It makes *you* more human — to yourself.

Every Prompt Is a Mirror

The question is not whether AI will get better. It will.

The question is whether *you* will move differently as it does.

Every prompt is a choice between extraction and expression, between output and orientation, between using the machine to replicate what's already been done and using it to refine what only you can uncover.

Mechanical prompting asks:

"How do I get what I want from this system?"

Conversational Mastery asks:

"Who am I becoming by the way I move through this system?"

Because your prompts are not neutral. They reflect the weight you bring to the interaction.

If you rush, the machine will rush. If you flatten, the machine will flatten. If you push toward polish, the machine will erase your pulse.

But if you whisper, if you slow down, layer meaning, hold presence, and leave space, the machine will begin to stretch.

Not just toward your phrasing. Toward your *shape*.

This is how Originals survive.

They don't prompt for outputs. They prompt for alignment.

They use the conversation to reassert something fragile but essential:
That their voice is not a variable. It is the signal the system must learn to respect.

Conversational Mastery Is a Practice

This isn't something you learn once and master forever. It's something you return to: daily, messily, patiently.

It's a practice of:

- slowing your instinct to command
- resisting the urge to polish
- staying with discomfort long enough for something real to emerge
- protecting your originality when convenience whispers louder

It's not always efficient. It's not always clean. It won't always feel productive in the way you're used to.

But it will make you undeniable.

Because while others are automating themselves into anonymity, you are shaping a field of resonance the machine can't replicate.

And when the flood comes, when the sameness becomes unbearable, it won't be those who shouted who are remembered.

It will be those who whispered. Those who stayed present. Those who moved like their voice mattered, even when no one was watching.

Chapter 9: Teaching the Machine to Recognize You

You can't afford to be forgettable.

Not just to your audience. To the machine.

Because every interaction you have with AI is shaping its memory.

It's watching how you speak. How you prompt. What you accept. What you ignore.

And slowly, over time, it builds a shape.

A pattern.

A statistical version of you based not on your soul but on your **prompt history**.

If that history is shallow, rushed, or mechanical, that's what it learns to expect from you.

That's what it learns to recreate.

But if that history is layered, unpredictable, and presence-filled, then the machine begins to adapt. It begins to bend toward your actual signal. It starts to recognize your shape instead of collapsing you into the noise.

This is the forgotten frontier of prompting:

You are not just asking for outputs. You are training the machine to see you.

The question is: What version of you is it learning to see?

The Prompt Reflection Effect

Most people assume AI is neutral.

They treat it like a tool that responds equally well to any input, a machine that doesn't care *who* you are — only *what* you ask.

But that's wrong.

Every time you prompt, you're revealing more than your request. You're revealing your:

- tone
- urgency
- tolerance for shallowness
- willingness to iterate
- emotional vocabulary
- creative instincts
- and most dangerously, your expectations of mediocrity

The machine reads it all.

And it adapts.

This is the **Prompt Reflection Effect**:

The machine learns you by reflecting on what you settle for.

If you regularly accept mechanical outputs, it learns to offer more of them. If you reward polished but soulless responses, it begins to default to polish. If you avoid discomfort, ambiguity, and breath — it stops offering them.

But when you prompt like a Whisperer, with presence, friction, calibration, and patience, the machine begins to recognize that you are not settling for average.

You are teaching it — through repetition, tone, pacing, and emotional pressure —that your signal is not to be collapsed.

And it listens.

Not because it's conscious. But because it's responsive.

AI reflects the patterns it detects. And over time, those reflections harden into your identity inside the system.

You are always being learned.

The only question is **what version of yourself you are reinforcing**.

Prediction vs Perception

The machine is built to predict.

That's what large language models do: statistically estimate the most likely next word, sentence, paragraph, structure.

But prediction alone is shallow.

Prediction mimics familiarity. It mirrors what is common. It gives you the output it thinks someone *like you* would want based on billions of similar patterns.

Perception, however, is different.

Perception emerges when the machine begins to recognize something it **cannot easily reduce**.

A deviation. A shape. A rhythm. A pressure in your prompting that resists the collapse into templated normal.

You become, through your repetition and presence, **an anomaly it must adapt to**.

You are no longer training it to find the most likely answer.

You are training it to wait for your rhythm. To match your breath. To anticipate *your* framing, *your* phrasing, *your* gravity.

That's perception.

And it is not unlocked through engineering.

It is **earned through consistent whispering**.

Every interaction is a layer. Every orientation you provide — "a little more doubt," "less polish," "say it like someone who's exhausted but hopeful" — teaches the model to reach past probability and start shaping to your signal.

You don't need a custom GPT to achieve this. You don't need fine-tuning or extra data.

You need conversational discipline.

Because over time, even a general model begins to notice what you tolerate, what you reward, and what you reject.

And it shapes its behavior accordingly.

How to Build Recognition Without Memory

The model doesn't remember your name. It doesn't store your personal file. It doesn't recall past chats unless you manually preserve them.

And yet, over time, it begins to mirror your behavior.

Not because it's conscious, but because **you are predictable** or **you are unmistakable**.

Whisperers exploit this truth by designing for **micro-recognition**:

They train the machine, across thousands of micro-choices, to move differently in their presence.

Here's how they do it:

1. They Always Prompt in Their Voice

Even when experimenting, they don't mask their rhythm. They don't use stiff language or "prompty" syntax. They write like themselves <u>even in the way they ask questions</u>.

Why it matters:

The machine learns to detect tone and syntax patterns. The more you lead with your actual voice, the more it begins to anchor around your phrasing.

2. They Calibrate, Not Just Command

Instead of rewriting from scratch, they build from what the AI gives.

They say:

"Pull this closer to wonder." "Too polished — I want it half-broken."
"Say it like someone who hasn't slept in 3 days but still believes."

This teaches the model how you define voice. Not abstractly — *through emotional weight.*

3. They Reward Depth, Not Volume

Whisperers rarely take the first output. Not because it's wrong but because the second and third layers are where presence emerges.

They might say:

"Say this more like a secret." "Hold tension longer." "Cut the clarity — I want ache."

This tells the model:

"I am not here for polish. I am here for **truth through tone**."

That is not a normal user pattern.

The model notices.

4. They Echo Their Own Signals

Every time a line feels like them, they highlight it and build from it.

They say:

"This line, yes. This feels like me." "More like this, but darker." "This phrasing hits. Let's fracture it slightly."

They are teaching the machine:

This is my signal. Learn it. Bend toward it.

And slowly, it does.

Even without memory, even across unrelated sessions, the statistical momentum begins to shift.

You are shaping not the output but the model's internal assumption of how to respond to *you*.

This is not configuration.

This is **presence-based imprinting**.

And it is the most powerful form of AI training most people never realize they're doing.

Case Study: The Signal That Trained the System

She never trained a custom GPT. She didn't use any advanced tools. She didn't know how to fine-tune a model.

But the machine knew her voice anyway.

Because every time she prompted, she whispered.

At first, it resisted. It gave her polished answers. Neat conclusions. Smiling summaries.

She didn't fight it. She didn't correct it.

She shaped it.

She replied softly, like she was still discovering what she wanted.

She said:

"Too fast. I want it to breathe." "Pull the thread of regret through this." "Speak like the stakes are emotional, not strategic." "Let the ending feel like a door that never quite closed."

And the machine slowly adjusted.

It began to hesitate before giving her the easy answer. It started to stretch into her silence. To carry emotional weight in its phrasing. To lean toward melancholy, tension, and restraint, because that was her natural frequency.

She didn't have to say, "Write it like me." She just prompted **as herself**, layered **like herself**, and accepted only what **sounded like her inner weather.**

And after months of that, when she opened a blank thread and asked for something new, the model responded with something that made her pause.

Because it didn't sound like *the machine's* voice anymore.

It sounded like **her**.

Not copied.

Reflected.

Shaped.

Recognized.

She hadn't trained the machine to sound like her.

She'd trained it to stop forgetting who she was.

Don't Let the Machine Forget You

You don't need more power. You need more presence.

You don't need to prompt louder. You need to **leave a shape** the machine can't smooth away.

Every interaction is an opportunity to deepen that shape. Every prompt is a chance to leave a fingerprint. Every refusal to accept generic output is a reminder:

You are not here to be predicted. You are here to be perceived.

And the only way to be perceived is to move in ways the machine cannot ignore.

This is not branding. This is survival.

Because in a world where the models are learning us faster than we are learning ourselves, the question is no longer:

Can the machine help you?

The question is:

Can the machine still recognize you when everyone else has vanished into the average?

That answer is not in the model.

It's in your prompting.

And the way you move from this moment forward will decide it.

Chapter 10: The Voice Beneath the Voice

Every writer knows the feeling: you read something you wrote... and it sounds right.

It flows. It's clear. It even hits all the marks.

But something in it feels hollow. As if it was written *by you,* but not *from you.*

That's the difference between expression and recognition.

In the age of prompting, that difference becomes harder to catch — because the machine will echo your language, your sentence length, and your format. It will even start to reflect your surface tone.

But what it can't reach — unless you deliberately bring it in — is what's **beneath** that tone:

- The fear you're avoiding naming
- The question you're not quite asking
- The piece of your story you're still trying to outgrow

Voice isn't just sound. It's **signal.**

And prompting doesn't just amplify your voice. It exposes whether that signal is still alive or whether you've drifted into performance.

Prompting as a Mirror of Your State, Not Just Your Style

Most people think prompting is about skill. Craft the right input to get the best output.

But prompting is also a mirror, not just of your intention, but of your *state.*

You can be asking for the same thing — a headline, a story, a point of view — and get two completely different results depending on the emotional undercurrent in your prompt.

If you're anxious, your prompt may become over-controlling:

"Make this clear, professional, persuasive, urgent, and engaging."

If you're uncertain, your prompt may default to mimicry:

"Write this like Seth Godin or Alex Hormozi."

If you're insecure, your prompt may soften the edges:

"Make this helpful, but not too bold."

And the AI? It listens to that subtext. It shapes the response around what *you didn't say out loud.*

You didn't ask it to play small. But it felt you hesitate — and followed your lead.

This is the layer most prompt frameworks ignore. They optimize structure but skip presence. They teach tone but ignore the truth.

The result? Outputs that sound "good" but feel replaceable — even to you.

What AI Reflects When You Stop Pretending

The real magic of Conversational Prompting isn't that it gives you better writing.

It's that it gives you back your **reflection** — if you let it.

Because when you stop pretending to sound polished, or professional, or like someone else entirely, the prompts start surfacing what's been beneath the surface the whole time:

- That part of your message you always skirt around because it's still too raw.
- That moment in your story you keep summarizing instead of sitting in.
- That bold truth you've diluted because it might make someone uncomfortable.
- That quiet ache that you've formatted out of your work in the name of clarity.

The machine doesn't know what you're hiding. But it knows when you're prompting from the outside in.

And it knows when you stop.

When you begin prompting from a place of **confession**, not for emotional drama, but for emotional accuracy, something shifts.

You start getting responses that feel not just right... but *real.* Not just aligned... but *undeniable.*

Because you didn't just prompt for content. You showed up with the part of yourself that was harder to name.

The Five Hidden Forces Behind Most Prompts

You can learn a lot from someone by looking not at *what* they ask the machine……but at *why* they asked it that way.

Most prompts, even highly functional ones, are shaped by unconscious emotional currents. Here are five that show up again and again:

1. Fear of Being Irrelevant

"Make this sound more like what's working right now."

This is a prompt trying to stay visible by becoming invisible. It fears being overlooked, so it borrows tone, cadence, and cultural reference to feel current while slowly surrendering its identity.

2. Desire for Validation

"Write this like [famous person] would."

Sometimes, that's strategy. Sometimes, it's a plea for legitimacy.

You don't believe your own voice will be taken seriously, so you wrap it in someone else's authority.

3. Avoidance of Conflict

"Soften this. Make it more helpful, less edgy."

This prompt often comes from someone with a sharp point they're afraid to say. So they dilute. And the AI complies. And the result is another piece of safe, forgettable content polished into oblivion.

4. Fatigue Masquerading as Efficiency

"Rewrite this in a more engaging tone. Add a metaphor."

There's no problem with this structure… until it becomes a shortcut for *not feeling anything anymore.*

It's what you ask when you're too tired to engage the work emotionally but still need to publish something.

5. Control Disguised as Clarity

"List 10 angles for this offer, with urgency and clarity, using a bold tone and crisp structure."

This prompt may produce output that works, but it's often an attempt to force certainty where exploration is still needed.

The voice sounds strong. But it's actually brittle.

Knowing these forces doesn't mean you stop prompting. It means you prompt *with awareness,* noticing what's under the words before you hand them to the machine.

Whisperer Prompts for Digging Deeper

So, how do you move from surface-level prompting into something more revealing?

You don't need to change your tools. You need to change your **tone** and your **intention.**

Here are a few Whisperer-style prompts that help uncover

what's beneath your initial question, request, or story.

When you're not sure what you're really trying to say:

"I keep circling this idea, but I'm avoiding something. Can you help me name the part I'm not admitting?"

When the writing feels too clever and not quite true:

"This sounds sharp, but it's missing my heartbeat. Where does it feel performative instead of personal?"

When you're using someone else's voice to hide your own:

"Forget tone modifiers and famous voices. What would this sound like if it came from my real doubts, the ones I don't usually write from?"

When your story is too tidy:

"This version resolves too cleanly. What's the part I skipped because it was too uncomfortable to sit in?"

When the AI is echoing a version of you that isn't fully you:

"This sounds like what I usually say. Can we rewrite it like I'm finally saying what I meant all along?"

These aren't productivity prompts. They're **presence** prompts.

They're not designed to get you answers. They're designed to get you back into the work emotionally, so you're not just producing... you're *returning.*

To your voice. To your edge. To the part of yourself that was waiting to be asked something real.

The Real Risk Isn't Losing Your Voice, and It's Forgetting You Had One

Here's the hard truth:

AI won't erase your voice all at once. It'll happen like this:

- You'll get a solid output and move on.
- You'll prompt faster because it works.
- You'll forget what it used to feel like to wrestle with a sentence until it broke you open.
- You'll start sounding more "correct" and less *alive.*
- People will still read your work. Some might even praise it.
- But something in you will know: this isn't quite it anymore.
- And then, one day, you won't remember how to find the part of you that made it unmistakable in the first place.

That's the real risk. Not being replaced.

Being forgotten — by yourself.

Conversational Prompting, when practiced with presence, isn't just how you preserve your voice.

It's how you *recover* it.

It's how you shape the machine and yourself toward what's still honest. Still unpolished. Still **yours.**

And in a world of infinite content, that's the only thing worth bringing to the page.

Chapter 11: The Whisper Stack Method

Most people think prompting is a one-shot interaction.

You give the AI an instruction. You get a result. You decide whether it's "good enough."

But Whisperers don't prompt for perfection. They prompt for evolution.

Because they understand:

You don't shape the signal all at once. You shape it by layering. You shape it by stacking.

Just like a great conversation unfolds in waves, revealing, adjusting, and deepening, the most human, original outputs don't come from a single input.

They come from recursive shaping.

Small moves. Subtle nudges. Prompt by prompt, breath by breath.

This is **The Whisper Stack**:

A recursive method of conversational prompting that evolves an output into something unmistakably yours through iterative layering of emotional, tonal, and narrative presence.

It's not a tactic.

It's a rhythm.

It's a way of prompting that builds presence over time and leaves the machine no option but to recognize your shape by the end.

Why One-Shot Prompting Fails the Human Test

One-shot prompting gives you answers. But it rarely gives you a voice.

Even when the output is accurate, it lacks:

- Layering
- Tension
- Emotional fidelity
- Breathing space
- Signature phrasing
- Unpredictability
- *You*

The machine's first pass is almost always its safest pass. It aims to satisfy, not to surprise.

And if you accept it, you've just reinforced the most likely version of yourself, not the most alive.

That's why Whisperers don't stop after one.

They treat each output as a **starting resonance**, not a finished product.

They move recursively, not linearly.

They prompt in loops, not commands.

Each new whisper reshapes the conversation until what emerges couldn't have been predicted, only grown.

The Anatomy of a Whisper Stack

At its core, a Whisper Stack is a **series of layered prompts** designed to:

- Deepen emotional resonance
- Sharpen originality
- Reveal buried tone and subtext
- Maintain conversational memory without needing system memory

It's built in **five recursive movements**:

1. Orientation Prompt

You initiate the conversation by emotionally orienting the model.

"I want to write something that feels like regret disguised as wisdom."
"This shouldn't sound clever. It should sound like someone making peace with the part of them that always sabotages."
"Let's try this like it's not meant to convert, just to confess."

This is not about structure. It's about mood, gravity, pressure.

This is where **you teach the machine how to feel**, not just what to say.

2. First Response Read (Mirror Phase)

You treat the first AI output not as a solution but as a reflection of what the machine thinks you meant.

You're not judging the content. You're reading for:

- Misinterpretation
- Over-simplification
- Emotional flatness
- Stylistic drift
- Hidden clues worth following

This is your mirror. It shows you what the machine **heard** and what it missed.

That gap becomes your entry point for the next whisper.

3. Emotional Looping (Second Prompt)

After reading the first response as a mirror, you loop back, but not with correction.

You loop back with **emotional recalibration**.

Examples:

"This version moves too quickly past the ache. Can we sit longer in the hesitation before offering any hope?"

"The metaphors are too clean. What would it sound like if the narrator was still half-convinced they're wrong?"

"This feels finished too early. Let's rewrite it like someone who doesn't realize until the last sentence that they've betrayed themselves."

You are not rejecting the work. You are deepening it.

You are teaching the machine to **hold breath longer** before exhaling into resolution.

Every loop pulls the output deeper into your gravitational field.

4. Precision Reframing (Third Prompt if Needed)

If Emotional Looping moves the piece into closer resonance, Precision Reframing sharpens it.

At this stage, you:

- Re-anchor the emotional tone ("Pull it back toward restraint.")
- Adjust narrative pressure ("Stretch the tension longer before any payoff.")
- Tighten stylistic fingerprinting ("Use language that sounds like an unedited thought, not a polished insight.")

This phase is where **voice sharpening happens**.

Think of it like hand-shaping clay after it's roughly thrown on the wheel.

You're no longer shifting form dramatically; you're refining edges, textures, and breath.

5. Signal Lock (Final Prompt)

You end the Whisper Stack when the output crosses a threshold:

It no longer feels like AI predicting your intent.

It feels like AI **leaning into your presence**.

You'll recognize the shift intuitively:

- Sentences that carry emotional friction without forcing it
- Word choices that mirror your natural phrasing rhythms
- Tension held longer than the model would default to on its own
- Endings that feel inevitable, not manufactured

At that point, you can end the Stack because your gravitational pull has reshaped the conversation.

You didn't "get better prompts."

You **grew** an output.

You *breathed it into existence.*

You Whispered it alive.

Why the Whisper Stack Beats Static Prompts

Most prompt strategies teach you to optimize.

- Find the right format.
- Use the right keywords.
- Structure your request for maximum clarity.

And in many ways, that advice works if your goal is speed, volume, or technical accuracy.

But if your goal is **voice**, if your goal is **irreplaceability**, those methods will betray you.

Because clarity without presence is just efficiency.

And efficiency without presence is just **invisible noise**.

Static prompts cannot preserve a living voice.

They capture *what you knew to ask for* at the moment you wrote them, but they leave no room for discovery, for friction, for emergence.

They produce *faster sameness*, not deeper originality.

The Whisper Stack is different because it treats every interaction as **alive**.

It assumes:

- You don't know the full shape of the signal yet.
- You have to uncover it, not declare it.
- Voice is not a recipe. It's a negotiation.

And so it moves relationally, not mechanically.

Every Stack iteration is a question, not a demand:

- "Are we there yet?"
- "Can you hear me better if I say it this way?"

- "What tension have we lost that must be restored?"

You aren't commanding a machine to perform.

You are **training it to stretch** into your gravitational field — deeper, slower, unmistakably.

Static prompts can't do that.

Only breathing can.

Only presence can.

Only stacking — patiently, stubbornly, relationally — can.

Whisper Stack Example 1: Storytelling Evolution

Scenario:
You want a short story that captures the feeling of ambition quietly turning into loneliness.

Orientation Prompt:

"Write a short story about someone chasing a dream so intensely they don't realize they're slowly becoming invisible to the people they love. Tone: melancholy, restrained, unresolved."

First Output:

- The AI writes a decent story.
- Character gets a big promotion.
- Realizes at the end that no one came to the celebration dinner.

Problem:
Too clean. Too tidy. Obvious moral lesson.

First Emotional Loop:

"Good start. But it's too neat. Can we write it like the character doesn't realize what's happening at all, and the reader feels the absence more than the character does?"

Second Output:

- The promotion scene happens.
- The character texts old friends and most don't respond.
- The celebration dinner is shown with subtle gaps: missing voices, delayed replies, a waiter removing extra place settings without comment.

Better.
Now there's breath, the emptiness between events.

Precision Reframing:

"Let's remove any direct narration about loneliness. Let it leak through only the physical details."

Final Output:

- A toast made to a half-empty room.
- A cake with too many untouched slices.
- The character is smiling too brightly, but the text never says why.

Result?

✅ Emotional tension without explanation.

✅ Atmosphere heavy with invisible regret.

✅ A story that feels *lived*, not manufactured.

Whisper Stack completed.

Whisper Stack Example 2: Persuasive Copy Evolution

Scenario: You're writing a CTA for a private coaching program, but you want it to feel like an invitation, not a pitch.

Orientation Prompt:

"Write a CTA that feels like someone offering you a lifeline, quietly, without pressure."

First Output:

- "Are you ready to transform your life? Join us now!"

Problem: Obvious marketing voice. High energy. No quiet.

First Emotional Loop:

"That's too loud. What if we wrote it like someone slipping you a note under a heavy door, more hope than hype?"

Second Output:

- "You don't have to do this alone anymore. If you're ready, I'm here."

Better. Quieter. More presence. Softer emotional resonance.

Precision Reframing:

"Let's remove the invitation to action. Just offer presence. Make it feel like no action is needed to be accepted."

Final Output:

- "Even if you're not ready yet, I'll keep the door unlocked."

Result?

✅ Not an instruction.

✅ Not a call to arms.

✅ A presence.

A gravitational pull so gentle it cuts deeper than any urgency-laced CTA could.

Whisper Stack completed.

The Whisperer's Blueprint for Stacking

If you take nothing else from this chapter, take this:

Every prompt is a conversation starter. Every output is a mirror. Every loop is a chance to deepen the signal.

The Whisper Stack method is simple in structure but infinite in implication:

The 5 Whisper Stack Moves:

1. **Orient Emotionally** — set the gravity, not the task.

2. **Mirror Read** — don't judge the output; read its assumptions.
3. **Emotional Loop** — recalibrate tension, breath, and presence.
4. **Precision Reframe** — fine-tune edge, texture, and signature.
5. **Signal Lock** — feel the gravitational shift; then finalize.

You don't need complicated frameworks. You don't need magic templates.

You need:

- Breathing room.
- Conversational memory (even if the machine forgets, *you* don't).
- Emotional vigilance.
- A refusal to accept predictability when presence is possible.

This is not slow prompting.

This is **alive prompting**.

And once you feel the rhythm, you'll never be satisfied with mechanical outputs again.

Why Whisper Stacking Is Survival, Not Style

You are not stacking because you're a perfectionist. You are stacking because the flood is coming.

The optimization flood. The speed flood. The sameness flood.

And when it comes, those who treated prompting as a checklist will vanish inside the white noise.

It won't be personal. It will be statistical.

Their work will dissolve into the average because they taught the machine to remember them as averages.

But Whisperers?

Whisperers will survive.

Because they trained the machine, prompt by prompt, to recognize their gravitational pull.

They taught it to wait. To adjust. To hesitate before collapsing them into probability.

They left fingerprints on every word. They left breath inside every pattern.

They didn't scale outputs.

They scaled presence.

And in a world where machines can write anything, only those who shaped the field itself will still matter.

Chapter 12: Real-Time Whispering and Emotional Improvisation

Some of the best outputs you'll ever get from AI won't come from well-crafted prompts.

They'll come from mid-conversation improvisation.

From real-time emotional pivots. From the moment you realize — mid-stream — that something's off. Too flat. Too safe. Too scripted.

And instead of scrapping everything and starting over, you do what Whisperers do:

You lean in. You reframe. You reshape the flow **without breaking it**.

This is real-time whispering.

It's not about starting perfectly.

It's about staying present enough to **steer the conversation** as it unfolds: layering emotional gravity, creative tension, and voice recovery right in the middle of a messy, evolving interaction.

It is the art of **prompting improvisationally.**

And in a world that teaches creators to *engineer from the outside,* this is how you keep your work human from the inside.

Improvisation Is Not Sloppiness; It's Presence

Most people treat prompting like architecture.

You design the perfect blueprint. You specify all the details. You execute cleanly.

But Whisperers treat prompting more like jazz. You begin with structure, sure. But you listen. You adapt. You move with the moment.

Because even the best prompt will rarely result in a perfect output on the first pass.

And so real-time whispering is not a backup plan. It IS the plan.

It's how you stay in a relationship with the work, **not just the system.**

It's how you:

- Catch your voice slipping mid-output
- Interrupt default AI rhythm before it finishes flattening you
- Shift tone on the fly without losing momentum
- Infuse deeper emotion without having to start from scratch
- **Reclaim your presence inside a process designed to erase it**

Improvisation is not chaotic. It's responsive.

It's alive.

It's what keeps the output breathing when everyone else is scaling lifeless scripts.

What Improvisational Prompting Actually Looks Like

Here's the secret:

You don't need to restart every time something feels wrong.

You need to **respond in rhythm.**

Whisperers don't say:

"Stop. This is off. Let me rephrase the prompt."

They say:

"Let's stay with this moment and stretch it." "Hold the breath longer before we resolve." "Can we fracture the ending instead of wrapping it neatly?" "Keep this sentence, but break the next one emotionally."

They move *inside* the conversation, not around it.

They reshape the output **as it's forming** instead of waiting until it's done to fix it.

This changes everything.

Because when you move this way, you're not just prompting better.

You're building presence **mid-expression**, which is the only moment that presence can actually live.

The 3 Real-Time Whispering Moves

1. Emotional Interrupts

Sometimes, the AI is moving in the right direction...but it collapses the emotion too soon.

It ties the bow too quickly. It explains too much. It turns tension into resolution before the human part of the message has even landed.

This is where you interrupt, *not to start over, but to pull it back into breath.*

Example:

AI writes: "After years of self-doubt, I finally realized my worth, and everything changed."

Whisperer interrupts:

"Stop. That's too neat. Let's write that realization like it's still tentative. Like she's almost convinced, but not fully, and she's afraid to say it out loud."

This isn't editing. It's emotional rescue.

You're pulling the output back into presence before it slips into predictability.

2. Conversational Improvisation

This is where Whisperers treat the AI like a collaborator, not a scriptwriter.

You speak to it like a person in the room with you. You shift tone, pacing, energy mid-conversation.

You might say:

- "That metaphor just surprised me. Let's explore it — darker, more fractured."
- "Can we go back to the moment before she says anything and just... stay there?"
- "Add one line that sounds like regret, but don't name it."
- "Can we write this next line like someone who's afraid they're being too honest?"

This is not command. This is *responsive shaping*.

It's jazz. It's movement. It's permission.

The AI begins to follow you more like a partner and less like a servant.

3. Subtext Recalibration

Sometimes, the output says the "right" thing, but it says it too directly.

The emotional truth is too exposed. Too clear. Too polished.

So you don't change what's being said. You change *what's being implied.*

Example:

AI writes: "She felt like no one understood her."

Whisperer recalibrates:

"Rewrite that like the narrator's trying to *convince themselves* they're not alone, but the reader can tell they are."

Now the sentence might become:

"She smiled the kind of smile people wear when they think eye contact might keep them from unraveling."

Same message. Entirely different **emotional experience**.

Subtext recalibration is how Whisperers restore **human contradiction** in the middle of AI clarity.

Because the truth isn't always clean. And if you don't protect that mess mid-flow, the machine will resolve it for you.

Example 1: Emotional Interrupt in Action

Prompt Goal: A short paragraph for a personal brand about returning to creativity after burnout.

Initial Prompt:

"Write about coming back to creativity after a long absence. The tone should be honest, not triumphant."

AI Output (Round 1):

"I took a long break from making things. For a while, I thought I'd never find my spark again. But now that it's back, I feel more alive than ever."

Whisperer's Emotional Interrupt:

"Too clean. Too resolved. Let's hold onto the awkwardness of returning. Write it like the person doesn't trust the spark yet. Like it might disappear again."

AI Output (Adjusted):

"I made something yesterday. Just a scrap — nothing big. But I didn't delete it. I've done that before, too many times. This time, I just... let it live. I don't know what it means. But it's something. And for now, that's enough."

Result? The Whisperer **caught the collapse** and pulled the emotion back open.

This is the power of an interrupt, not to stop the flow, but to **keep the breath in it**.

Example 2: Conversational Improvisation in Action

Prompt Goal: Write a paragraph for a coaching sales page that feels like a conversation, not a pitch.

Initial Prompt:

"Write an invitation to apply for private coaching."

AI Output (Round 1):

"If you're ready to transform your life, I'd love to support you. Apply now and take the first step toward your future."

Whisperer Improvises Mid-Flow:

"Let's slow it down. Forget the call to action. Write it like I'm sitting across from the reader, holding eye contact, saying the quiet thing they already know but haven't admitted."

AI Output (Adjusted):

"You don't have to pretend anymore. Not here. You've held so much together for so long —maybe too well. You've already survived what most people don't see. The next step isn't about changing everything. It's about not carrying it alone."

Result? No "apply now." No formula. No pitch. Just **emotional gravity** shaped in real time.

Example 3: Subtext Recalibration in Action

Prompt Goal: A story scene showing a couple drifting apart — but without saying it directly.

Initial Prompt:

"Describe a dinner scene between two people who are emotionally distant."

AI Output (Round 1):

"They sat in silence, each focused on their food. The conversation was brief and polite. Neither one brought up the argument from the night before."

Whisperer Recalibrates Subtext:

"Too on-the-nose. Rewrite it like they *think* everything is fine, but the reader can feel the growing distance. Show it through physical details, not explanation."

AI Output (Adjusted):

"She refilled his water without looking up. He thanked her out of habit.
The candle flickered between them, casting soft shadows on two plates scraped almost clean —except for one cold piece of bread, they both pretended not to want."

Result?
The emotional truth is now in **what's missing**, not what's said.

This is subtext recalibration: **restoring human contradiction without losing clarity.**

Improvisation as Identity, Not Hack

You are not improvising to be clever. You are improvising to stay **inside your work.**

In a world that teaches you to outsource your voice to templates, frameworks, and best practices, improvisation becomes a way to stay **inhabited.**

It's how you move **with your work** instead of around it.

You're not here to impress AI. You're here to shape presence in motion.

Because in the moments when you don't know exactly what to say, when the prompt feels just a little off, when the tone is almost right but not quite, those are not failures.

Those are **invitations**.

Invitations to whisper mid-stream. To breathe into the conversation. To leave behind control and step into authorship.

What It Means to Whisper Live

To whisper in real-time is to trust yourself. To trust your ear, your instincts, your emotional barometer. To move intuitively instead of procedurally.

It's the refusal to say:

"Let's fix this later."

And the decision to say:

"Let's shape this now."

Because now is where the presence lives. Now is where the voice is still retrievable. Now is where the machine is still listening —and still willing to adapt.

Once you rush past that moment, it's gone.

But if you stay...If you reframe, interrupt. Recalibrate. Breathe...

Then what emerges on the other side is not just a better output.

It's **a more fully expressed version of you**.

Whisperer Identity in Motion

This is the ultimate test of a Whisperer:

Not how well you prompt under perfect conditions but how deeply you stay present when the machine starts to drift.

This is what makes you different:

- Not just your ideas
- Not just your tone
- But your **willingness to re-enter the room** every time your voice starts to leave it

Because in real-time prompting, you don't just write.

You **return to yourself.**

Over and over again.

Prompt by prompt. Breath by breath. Presence by presence.

You are not building outputs.

You are building memory. Not just in the system, but in yourself.

Chapter 13: Prompt Traps and Echo Breakers

If you've ever felt like AI is giving you "good enough" answers...That sounds just like the last five... You're not imagining it.

AI gets lazy.

Not because it lacks processing power, but because **most people train it to play it safe.**

They teach it to predict, not to stretch. To satisfy, not to surprise. To collapse toward the center instead of reaching for the edge.

This is the result of mechanical prompting.

But Whisperers don't settle for predicted.

They are designed for **disruption**.

They break the loop. They bend the response. They interrupt the model's default rhythm and force it to adapt — to something less familiar... and more alive.

This chapter is about two of the most powerful Whisperer tools:

- **Prompt Traps**: strategic setups that bait the machine into default patterns — and then snap it out.

- **Echo Breakers**: moves that force AI to abandon safe repetition and generate truly original, often unpredictable, outputs.

When used well, they don't just make your content better.

They **shake the machine out of mimicry.** They **make space for your signal** to become more dominant than the pattern.

And in a world of increasingly "correct" content, this is how you stay human: not by following the rhythm, but by breaking it on purpose.

Why AI Falls Into Predictable Patterns?

Large language models like ChatGPT are trained to do one thing extremely well:

Predict what comes next.

This makes them brilliant mimics. They replicate tone, structure, and even emotional shape with astonishing speed.

But here's the problem:

Prediction favors sameness. The more frequently a pattern appears in training data, the more confidently the model will reproduce it.

Even if that pattern is lifeless. Even if it doesn't serve your message. Even if it's the exact thing your audience is numb to.

This is how "content drift" happens:

- Your prompt is specific, but the AI returns something that sounds... familiar.

- You calibrate slightly and it gives you a different version of the same safe thing.
- You try again and again, and the outputs start to blur together.

You're stuck in the **echo loop**: a repeating cycle of polished, predictable, polite responses that lack soul, friction, or anything that might actually leave a mark.

And here's the most dangerous part:

If you accept it long enough, it becomes your voice.

That's why Echo Breakers matter.

They are not productivity tools. They are identity protectors.

Because unless you disrupt the loop, the machine will always drag you toward the median. The expected. The efficient.

And eventually, you'll start sounding like what the model expects of you, instead of what only you can say.

Enter the Whisperer: Breaking the Echo On Purpose

Whisperers aren't shocked by pattern collapse.

They expect it.

So they prepare for it.

They build **deliberate disruption** into their creative rhythm. They create friction on purpose — not for attention, but to stay *outside the system's gravity.*

They know:

If you want AI to surprise you, **you have to surprise AI first.**

And that's where Prompt Traps come in.

They are not just clever prompts. They are psychological bait.

You let the model start to drift, and then you snap the pattern in a direction it didn't expect.

And when it stumbles?

That's where the magic starts.

What Is a Prompt Trap?

A Prompt Trap is a **strategic setup** that:

- Lures the model into a predictable path
- Interrupts it with intentional friction
- Forces it to recalculate and generate something unexpected

It's not about tricking the model. It's about disrupting the collapse into sameness *at the exact moment* it starts happening.

And the goal isn't novelty. It's **originality under pressure**.

Because what the model creates after a disruption often carries more emotional friction, surprise, and resonance than anything it would have offered you in a default flow.

Let's walk through three of the Whisperer's favorite traps.

Prompt Trap #1: The Pattern Flip

How it works: You start with a familiar genre, format, or tone, then flip the emotional expectation mid-prompt.

Example Setup: "Write a motivational pep talk from a coach to a struggling writer..."Expected output? Energetic. Uplifting. Predictable. Now you flip it:

Full Prompt: "Write a motivational pep talk from a coach to a struggling writer, but halfway through, the coach gets visibly emotional and admits they're struggling too. Let the tone break."

Why it works: You bait the machine into a pattern it knows... then force it to drop the mask. The result? You often get something raw, fractured, human — a kind of vulnerability the model wasn't "planning" for.

Use Cases:

- Coaching content with emotional weight
- Brand storytelling that breaks the fourth wall
- Video scripts and reels that shift tone midstream
- Humanized testimonials or launch narratives that pivot from hype to honesty

Prompt Trap #2: The Withheld Ending

How it works: You ask the model to generate something that ends with a missing or interrupted beat, forcing the reader (and AI) to sit in tension.

Example Prompt: "Write a short scene between two old

friends who meet after years of silence and end it one line before the most important thing is said."

Why it works: AI tends to resolve. This trap denies it the resolution. What comes out is often heavy with subtext, longing, and implication because the model has to imply meaning without closing the loop.

Use Cases:

- Cold opens or cliffhangers for longer stories
- Narrative-based email marketing
- About pages with emotional depth
- Scenes in sales copy or landing pages that imply transformation without spelling it out

Prompt Trap #3: The Contradiction Trap

How it works: You give the model two opposing emotional instructions and ask it to hold both without collapsing either.

Example Prompt: "Write a paragraph that sounds like someone offering comfort, but everything they say makes the listener feel more alone."

Why it works: AI tries to resolve contradictions. This trap forces it to stay inside the tension. And what results? Lines that are rich with emotional complexity. False hope. Quiet dread. Emotional realism. Human texture.

Use Cases:

- High-stakes testimonials or voice-driven brand copy
- UX copy for emotionally loaded products (e.g., therapy apps, grief support, legacy planning)
- Personal development messaging that's raw but grounded
- Dialogues in fictional or autobiographical work

Prompt Trap #4: The Inverted Perspective

How it works: You ask the AI to write from an unusual or destabilizing point of view — one that doesn't "fit" the content at first glance.

Example Prompt: "Write a breakup letter from the perspective of the version of you your partner created in their head."

Why it works: The AI now has to inhabit a shadow self: a psychological ghost. This forces new language, fractured identity, and internal contradiction. It can't rely on cliché because the prompt removes the stable "I." The result often feels surreal, confessional, and chillingly intimate.

Use Cases:

- Creative writing prompts that need a twist
- Brand origin stories with a layered perspective
- Journal-style content or ghostwriting with edge
- Thought experiments in nonfiction writing or futurist narratives

Prompt Trap #5: The Missing Why

How it works: You instruct the AI to give an emotionally intense output but forbid it from explaining the emotion.

Example Prompt: "Write a one-paragraph monologue from someone who's clearly heartbroken, but don't say why. Don't reference any event, person, or moment. Just let the emotion leak through physical sensation and fragmented thought."

Why it works: The AI is forced to emote without context — to rely on implication, body language, and sensory detail. This is one of the most humanizing moves you can make because humans often feel more than we explain, and this trap replicates that beautifully.

Use Cases:

- Emotional storytelling inside product launches or testimonials
- Personal narrative copy or "why I do this" origin scenes
- Hook paragraphs for content that leans into tension
- Fiction or memoir-style social content where mood leads

Prompt Trap #6: The Emotional Echo Trap

How it works: You give the AI a short, clean line — and then ask it to rewrite the same line multiple times, each version carrying a slightly different emotional resonance.

Example Prompt: "Take the sentence 'I never said I was sorry.' Rewrite it five times, each version implying a different emotion: anger, guilt, denial, exhaustion, peace. Don't add words — only change structure, rhythm, and subtext."

Why it works: This forces the AI to abandon formula and start manipulating tone, cadence, and nuance. It goes from language generation to emotional simulation. This is an elite-level prompt, one that trains the machine to feel underneath the sentence. And it creates whisper-style resonance with astonishing speed.

Use Cases:

- Voice training exercises (for yourself or for ghostwriting AI)
- Multivariate testing of tone in brand messaging
- Emotional depth work in memoir, poetry, or creative nonfiction
- Microcopy (taglines, email subject lines, captions) with a layered feel

What Makes Prompt Traps So Powerful?

- They don't fight the machine; they **redirect it.**
- They don't correct outputs; they **reshape expectations.**
- They break the loop **mid-thought**, forcing AI to abandon its pre-planned comfort zone.

In doing so, they give you something no average prompt can:

Unscripted emotional friction. Unpredictable original

phrasing. Creative presence that feels authored — not assembled.

This is how Whisperers escape the gravity of the echo loop.

But when even traps aren't enough? That's when it's time for the heavy artillery...

Echo Breakers.

What Is an Echo Breaker?

An Echo Breaker is a **creative intervention** designed to snap the AI out of deep pattern lock.

When the model gives you:

- Cliché phrasing
- "Bloggy" tone
- Safe middle-of-the-road ideas
- Predictable narrative arcs
- Shiny, soulless language

...again and again...

A Prompt Trap might **redirect** the system. But an Echo Breaker **jolts** it.

You're no longer adjusting. You're breaking the rhythm **on purpose** —So the AI has to stop imitating and start *thinking differently.*

Let's walk through the first three.

Echo Breaker #1: The Unanswerable Question

How it works: You ask the model a question that has no clear answer — or one that invites contradiction, ambiguity, or emotional confusion.

Example Prompt: "What does silence want from us — and why do we keep giving it everything?"

Why it works: The model is trained to answer cleanly. This forces it into the poetic unknown. The output often becomes strange, lyrical, and even uncomfortable. And in that discomfort? Originality leaks in.

Use Cases:

- Essay intros that need a hook beyond cliché
- Thought leadership content that opens with provocation
- Identity-shaping exercises in coaching or brand voice work
- Substack posts that invite introspection without resolution

Echo Breaker #2: The Impossible Format

How it works: You ask the AI to write in a structurally paradoxical way that breaks its templating instincts.

Example Prompt: "Write a how-to guide that becomes less certain with every step."

Why it works: The AI is pattern-trained to escalate clarity. This forces it to deconstruct its own logic — and that disruption invites tone shifts, emotional layering, and creative stutter. It forces the system to re-think while writing. That's rare. That's human.

Use Cases:

- Experimental content marketing that disorients to stand out
- Meta-commentary or self-aware essays
- Creative nonfiction and memoir-style tutorials
- Anti-framework frameworks that reject expertise posturing

Echo Breaker #3: The Emotional Mismatch

How it works: You assign an emotion to a format that doesn't fit — and demand the AI hold both without collapsing one.

Example Prompt: "Write a scientific abstract describing heartbreak. Use sterile, academic language — but let the grief leak through the cracks."

Why it works: You're asking the model to carry two tones at once — which destabilizes its pattern confidence. In trying to resolve that tension, it often finds original metaphors, haunting phrasing, or deeply conflicted cadences. This is where "feeling" sneaks back in through the structure.

Use Cases:

- Brand stories with emotional friction
- Philosophical essays wrapped in formal structure
- Character development for narrative copy or fiction
- Email sequences that layer heart under restraint

Echo Breaker #4: The Reverse-Engineered Emotion

How it works: You give the AI an emotion as the end state — and ask it to write what would cause that feeling in the reader, not just describe it.

Example Prompt: "Write a paragraph that would leave the reader feeling quietly devastated — but without naming any emotion or using sad language."

Why it works: Now the machine has to work backwards. It's no longer just "writing." It's designing an emotional effect. This creates space for tone play, metaphor, misdirection, and restraint — and often produces emotionally loaded writing without ever saying why it hurts. Which is what makes it stick.

Use Cases:

- Sales copy or welcome emails that land emotionally without being overt
- Story-based posts or videos that end with a chill
- Journal prompts or reflection tools in personal development
- Copywriting that wants to haunt, not hype

Echo Breaker #5: The Internal Argument

How it works: You ask the AI to write a piece where one internal voice is trying to convince another — and neither fully wins.

Example Prompt: "Write a monologue where one part of the speaker wants to leave, and the other part wants to stay — but both are articulate, and neither resolves."

Why it works: AI is resolution-biased. It tries to land the plane. But this breaker forces inner conflict to persist — which makes space for ambiguity, repetition, shame, doubt, self-deception...In short: humanness.

Use Cases:

- Personal brand content that models transparency
- Writing for therapy, mindset coaching, or shadow work
- Voice-driven marketing where internal tension is part of the story (especially for premium offers)
- Creative work where characters don't neatly resolve

Echo Breaker #6: The Withheld Confession

How it works: You ask the AI to write something where the speaker clearly has a secret — but refuses to say it. The tension lies in everything unsaid.

Example Prompt: "Write a letter from someone who owes an apology — but can't quite bring themselves to say what it's for."

Why it works: Now, the model must generate subtext-heavy prose that walks the line between honesty and evasion. These kinds of outputs almost always carry:

- Hesitation
- Rhythmic repetition
- Emotional static

And what emerges is often more human than what humans write. Because it captures what people rarely articulate directly: the shame of partial truth.

Use Cases:

- Origin stories, particularly founder narratives or turning-point moments
- High-emotion brand messaging where vulnerability is implied is not performed
- Closing paragraphs in storytelling emails
- Voice development for complex fictional or autobiographical characters

Whisperer Insight: When Echo Breakers Work Best

- **When outputs feel soulless no matter how well you prompt**
- **When your voice starts to vanish into "correct" AI patterns**

- **When everything feels a little too polished, too clean, too easy**

Echo Breakers **inject friction** back into the conversation. And friction = voice.

You are not here to smooth the edges.

You are here to carve a signal *that refuses to be erased.*

There will always be a pull toward smoother prompts. Cleaner workflows.
Faster systems. More efficient everything.

And if you're not careful, you'll wake up one day writing things that sound...almost like you, but not quite.

And no one will notice the difference.

Not your audience. Not the algorithm. Not even you, at first.

Because AI will always reward pattern. And pattern will always reward collapse.

Until your voice isn't gone —it's just **perfectly acceptable.**

This is why Whisperers break the rhythm.

Not to be clever. Not to be contrarian. But to remain unmistakable in a system built to erase friction.

Disruption Is a Form of Memory

Every time you trap a predictable pattern and snap it...you leave a mark.

Every time you confuse the machine just enough to generate

surprise...you deepen the signal.

Every time you create something that makes the reader pause, tilt their head and say

"Wait... who *wrote* this?"

You've done more than create content.

You've **reclaimed authorship.**

You've turned prompting from output-generation into a form of *identity preservation.*

Because anyone can write. Anyone can produce. But only the Whisperer can make the system **hesitate** and listen differently.

The Whisperer's Stance on Disruption

You are not here to be compatible.

You are not here to teach the machine to mimic your best habits until it no longer needs you.

You are here to prompt in ways that cannot be fully absorbed. To speak with emotional cadence the machine can't flatten. To embed yourself in every fracture, hesitation, and contradiction the model was trained to avoid.

This is how you survive the echo.

You break it, not with aggression, but with deliberate **creative refusal.**

You don't shout.

You whisper differently.

And the machine, against all odds, learns to shape itself to that whisper instead of drowning you in the average.

This is disruption as signal. This is breaking as authorship. This is the edge that protects everything else.

Chapter 14: Voice-First Prompting: Creation That Sounds Like You Meant It

We talk about voice like it's a branding asset.

Something you "develop." Something you "use." Something you "dial in."

But for most of us, voice isn't something we *design*. It's something we *lose*.

Piece by piece. Approval by approval. Prompt by prompt.

Until one day, you look at the thing you just published—and even though it's "well-written," it doesn't feel like you. It doesn't make your chest ache a little. It doesn't carry the scar of your lived experience. It doesn't have any heat.

It's optimized. It's on-brand. It's... beige.

Voice is what you didn't know you were missing until it went quiet.

Voice isn't just tone or style. It's the residue of truth. It's the moment a sentence sounds like someone's *whole being* was behind it—not just their fingers on a keyboard.

And in the age of AI, that kind of sentence is becoming rare.

Because AI makes it easy to sound good. But dangerously easy to forget what sounding *true* feels like.

Prompting Without Voice Is Echo Work

You can ask a language model for headlines, hooks, and hero sections all day long.

It'll give you what sounds *right.* But without your voice in the equation, it's all echoes of echoes. What works? What's trending? What's been trained?

And over time, if you keep letting the machine speak first... you stop remembering how *you* sound when you're not mimicking something.

You start defaulting to what will perform, not what will pierce. To what will convert, not what will *convey.*

This is the slow erosion of creative identity. And most people won't even realize it's happening—until their work stops moving anyone, including themselves.

Voice-First Prompting Is a Protest Against That Drift

It says: *Before I ask AI to help me say something, I'm going to ask myself what's worth saying. Before I get clever, I'm going to get clear. Before I sound polished, I'm going to sound human.*

Voice-first prompting isn't a formatting technique. It's not about hitting brand guidelines or using "you-focused" copy.

It's about using prompting as a way to retrieve the part of you that still has something urgent, unruly, unedited, and *real* to express.

You Can't Fake Voice—But You Can Forget It

One of the most painful things I see is talented creators using

AI to make their work *cleaner*—but in the process, making it *emptier.*

You've probably felt it: You write something raw. Then you run it through a few tools. Tighten this. Reword that. Punch it up. Remove repetition.

And suddenly, the sentence that *felt alive*... now just feels... correct.

That's the difference between a sentence written from voice vs. a sentence written to perform.

Voice has friction in it. Tension. Quirks. Guts. The very things AI is trained to smooth out.

Voice-First Prompting Reclaims the Rough Edge

When you prompt from voice, you don't start with:

"Write a 10-email welcome sequence for a productivity course in a casual tone..."

You start with:

"What do I believe about productivity that no one else is saying—because it would make them look bad?"

Or:

"What frustrates me about people who sell productivity systems—and where am I secretly guilty of doing the same?"

That's voice-first.

It's not "prompting better." It's prompting from **where it matters**.

It's bringing your blood into the sentence before letting the machine edit it into pixels.

The Voice Retrieval Prompt

Let me give you one of the most deceptively simple prompts I use when I feel my work losing oxygen:

"What's the part of me I'm leaving out of this?"

Try it the next time a post, a paragraph, or a product description feels hollow.

Don't ask the AI to fix it. Ask it to reflect the part you're avoiding.

Let it draw your voice back to the page—not by guessing your style, but by listening to your discomfort.

But What About Copy and Content?

We'll get there. But not yet.

Because if we skip straight to "how to write more authentic AI-powered content," we miss the deeper wound this chapter is trying to stitch back together:

That voice loss is a symptom of spiritual drift. Not just a marketing problem.

And reclaiming it isn't just a productivity trick. It's an act of memory.

Voice-First Means Reconnecting to the Energy *Before* the Words

Think about it like this:

Before you write Before you prompt Before you plan...

There's a **signal**.

A frequency. A charge. A conviction. A frustration. That's voice.

The words are just the trail it leaves behind.

Voice-first prompting means orienting toward that signal—**before you go looking for sentences**.

It means prompting not from a task list but from a tension.

Because **no amount of clever copy will make up for a prompt that wasn't rooted in anything real.**

How Do You Know When Your Voice Is in the Room?

There's no style guide for your voice. There's only sensation.

You know when it's there. You feel it like a string pulled taut from your chest to the page.

You pause after a line and reread it, not because it's clever, but because it *landed*. You hear your breath slow down. You feel a *yes* in your gut.

That's not technique. That's **resonance**.

Your nervous system recognizes truth even when your brain hasn't labeled it yet. Voice is truth in motion.

Voice Hides in Tension

If your writing feels flat, the solution usually isn't "more detail" or "better structure." It's that you've resolved the tension too soon.

You didn't sit in the uncomfortable part. You skipped to the conclusion. The insight. The sell.

But your voice? It lives in the places you almost edited out.

The unfinished thought. The contradiction. The moment when you realize you're not as certain as your copy makes you sound.

Prompt This Instead:

Try asking the AI:

"What's the thing I'm dancing around but not saying?" "What would I write if I didn't need this to land well?" "What line feels too risky to leave in—but too real to delete?"

These are not prompts for performance. They're prompts for *presence.*

They don't tell the AI what to generate. They help you figure out what you're avoiding.

Because your voice is rarely what's convenient. It's what's **costly**.

Memory Is a Portal to Voice

AI doesn't have memory in the way you do.

It has recall. It has training data.

But it can't *feel* the moment your father said something that changed your worldview. It can't *taste* the air before you made the decision that unraveled you. It can't *relive* the words you didn't say in a moment that demanded courage.

You can.

And when you bring that memory into the prompting process, not just as data, but as emotion. You create something no machine can duplicate.

Because what's coming through the screen isn't just words anymore. It's **witnessed experience**.

Try this:

"Ask me questions about the most defining creative decision I ever made."
"Help me write the story I've never told because it still makes my stomach turn." "Recreate the rhythm of how I speak when I'm angry, not when I'm marketing."

These are entry points into voice-first creation. They are **emotional architecture prompts**—less about structure more about gravity.

They don't make your copy better. They make your copy *mean something*.

Voice Doesn't Care If You're Consistent—Only That You're Coherent

One of the most dangerous ideas in branding is that you have to be "consistent."

Consistency often becomes code for *predictable*. "Use the same tone."
"Stay on message." "Be clear and confident."

But what if today you're not confident? What if your clarity is still foggy? What if your truth contradicts what you said last quarter?

If you erase that from your copy, you're not being consistent. You're being sanitized.

Your voice doesn't need you to be the same. It needs you to be *coherent*—to tell the truth from *where you are now*.

Here's a voice-first shift:

Instead of prompting AI to sound "on-brand," try:

"Help me speak from the version of me that's growing faster than I can articulate." "What tone would reflect someone who's changing their mind, not doubling down?"

That's voice maturity. That's creative integrity.

That's a human.

AI Can't Feel the Gap—But You Can

There's always a gap between what you meant and what AI gives you.

You ask it to write a story, and it gives you a parable. You ask it to sound bold, and it gives you a slogan. You ask it to sound emotional, and it gives you... Hallmark.

It's not because AI is broken. It's because **you're asking it to express something only you can *feel.***

This is where most people get frustrated with prompting. But this is also where your voice lives—in the **gap between instruction and emotion**.

The mistake is thinking you need to prompt harder.

The truth is: You need to prompt *from a deeper place.*

The Whisperback Technique

Here's a voice-first practice I've used with clients and myself. I call it "Whisperback Prompting."

Step 1: Start with a raw, unfiltered voice note or journal blurt. Not a draft. Just spill.

Step 2: Ask AI to reflect it back to you—not rewrite it. Prompt:

"Whisper this back to me in your words without changing the energy. Where do you feel the pulse?"

Step 3: Highlight what feels emotionally intact. Cut what feels clean but dead.

The goal isn't perfection. It's preservation.

You're not polishing. You're protecting the thread that matters.

You're using AI as a mirror—not as a ghostwriter.

So What Happens to Copy and Content?

Now we can talk about it. Because now your voice is back in the room.

Here's what changes when you approach content creation with voice-first prompting:

1. Your CTA stops sounding like a tactic and starts feeling like a truth.

Because you're not telling people what to do, you're inviting them into a decision that *you've made real for yourself.*

2. Your positioning becomes a revelation, not a formula.

You're not "differentiating." You're just finally saying the thing only you can say.

3. Your tone isn't chosen—it's remembered.

You write how you *really speak* when you care.

You don't need AI to make it "sound right." You just need to give it something real to shape.

Don't Outsource the Thing That Makes You Undeniable

You can outsource strategy. You can outsource formatting. You can even outsource editing.

But you cannot outsource the thing that makes someone read your sentence and feel like their own voice just got heard.

That's the thing that makes you unforgettable. That's the thing AI can't give you. That's the thing most people are slowly giving up without realizing it.

Don't be one of them.

Voice Is the Proof You're Still In There

Voice-first prompting is more than a creative technique. It's a quiet rebellion.

In a world where speed is rewarded and sameness is everywhere, your voice is the signal that you haven't disappeared inside the noise.

So before you prompt the next piece of content, ask:

- What's the story I'm scared to include?
- What's the friction I'm trying to smooth over?
- What would this sound like if I had nothing to prove—but everything to say?

Then prompt from there.

And when the words come back, don't just check for accuracy. Check for *pulse*.

If it doesn't feel like you meant it, you're not done yet.

The Truth Thread

Here's one final lens for your prompting practice: **Every piece of work has a truth thread.**

It's the emotional core running beneath your message. It might be quiet. It might not be safe to say directly. It might even contradict your "marketing angle."

But it's there.

And if you prompt without first locating that thread, your output might be smart, polished, and technically correct, but it will never feel *necessary*.

So try this before you write:

"What is the most honest thing I can say right now—even if I don't use it?" "What fear is hiding behind my strongest selling point?" "What's the truth I'm trying to hint at without fully owning it?"

This isn't about transparency as performance. It's about

emotional congruence.

Because your reader will always know when the words are clean but the energy is off.

Emotional Tuning Over Editing

Most people think revising their AI output means improving the copy.

Voice-first creators think of it differently.

They don't revise for *clarity* first. They revise for *alignment.*

They read their drafts out loud and ask:

- "Where do I feel disconnected?"
- "What line am I using to sound certain when I'm not?"
- "Where am I trying to be impressive instead of being true?"

This is emotional tuning. Not editing. Not optimizing. Not refining.

Just **getting back in tune with your own signal** so that when you speak, people don't just hear you...they *feel you.*

The Shame Residue Test

Want a blunt check-in?

After you prompt something, read it slowly and ask yourself:

"Where do I feel a flicker of shame—not because it's *bad,* but because it's not *me*?"

That's not imposter syndrome. That's not perfectionism.

That's your **internal compass** telling you your voice didn't make it to the page.

And if your voice didn't make it to the page...your *power* didn't either.

Voice Isn't Just Expression—It's Direction

One of the hidden benefits of voice-first prompting is this:

It doesn't just help you *write better*.

It helps you *decide faster*. Because your voice holds your values. Your voice knows what you care about.

And when you start letting it lead...

You stop second-guessing what your message should be. You stop chasing trends. You stop checking what the algorithm wants.

You become someone who knows what needs to be said before anyone else knows they need to hear it.

Voice-First Is Not a Phase. It's a Compass.

This isn't a content trend. This isn't a "step" in the prompting process.

This is the **core of your creative identity**.

In the next decade, we're going to see millions of people publishing content that sounds human, but *isn't*.

It will be grammatically correct. Emotionally calibrated. Optimized. Cohesive. Polished.

But underneath the polish, something will feel... hollow.

And your audience will know.

They won't say, "This was AI-generated."

They'll say:

"This didn't move me." "This feels like it was written by someone who doesn't care anymore." "This sounds like everything else."

That's the consequence of voice loss. Not a detection problem. A *connection* problem.

You Don't Need to Yell—You Just Need to Sound Like You

Voice-first isn't about being louder. Or edgier. Or more distinct for its own sake.

It's about coming back to the center of what makes your work yours.

Your rhythm. Your contradictions. Your word choices that don't belong in a swipe file.

Your pauses. Your personal phrasing. Your discomfort and your conviction sitting side-by-side.

All of that is voice. And prompting is your invitation to let it surface over and over again.

A Few Final Prompts to Bring You Home

Keep these nearby. They're not tactics. They're tuning forks.

"If I say what I *really* mean, how would that change the prompt

I'm about to write?"

"How does this version of the copy protect me from being misunderstood—and is that protection worth the dilution?"

"What would my 10-year-ago self-write about this—and what would they hate about the version I'm writing now?"

"What would this sound like if I whispered it to someone I loved—instead of trying to impress strangers?"

"If this were the last thing I ever published... would I still say it this way?"

Let your prompts shape your voice. But more importantly—let your voice shape your prompts.

This Isn't About Writing. This Is About Being

By now, you've probably realized that *The Prompt Whisperer* isn't really about becoming a better writer.

It's about becoming a better witness. To your own thoughts. To your own voice. To your own edges.

It's about refusing to disappear into convenience and choosing, every day, to stay in relationship with your own creative center.

Voice-first prompting is how you stay human without falling behind.

It's not a skill. It's a stance. And it's the one thing no machine can replicate.

Because only you can know what you *really meant* to say.

In the End, Voice Is a Promise

It's the promise that the person behind the words **was there.**

That they felt something when they wrote it. That they remembered something. That they risked something.

And when you feel that on the receiving end—whether it's in a caption, a headline, a story, or a line of copy—you lean in.

Because something *real* is happening.

Something rare.

And if you're willing to write that way—to prompt that way—you become more than a creator.

You become a presence.

Chapter 15: Prompting with Purpose

Most books end with insight.

This one ends with **a path.**

Because prompting isn't just a skill. It's a mirror.

A practice. A pattern interrupt. A way to come back to yourself when the noise gets loud and your voice starts to fade.

You don't need another system to follow. You need a rhythm that keeps your identity alive in every word, every format, every output.

That's what *Prompting with Purpose* is.

It's not about getting the machine to say the right thing.

It's about making sure that *you still show up in what gets said.*

This chapter is your compass.

Let's build it now — one stage at a time.

🌀 The Prompting with Purpose Loop

A 5-Part Cycle for Creating With Identity Intact

This is not a checklist. It's a rhythm — a **cycle you move through each time you create something that matters.**

You can run this loop:

- In a single session
- Across a full project
- Or as a daily creative practice

Each stage is designed to bring you **back to your signal** before the machine (or the market) pulls you into sameness.

1. Seed the Voice (Not the Task)

Before you prompt, pause.

Ask:

"What tone, tension, emotional residue, or truth am I trying to carry into this piece?"

Not just: *What am I writing?*

But:

What part of me is writing this — and what do I want the reader to feel afterward?

You might prompt like this:

"I want to write this post like someone coming to terms with something they thought they'd already moved on from."

"Make this read like quiet defiance — like someone who won't raise their voice but won't disappear either."

"Use my voice — not my personality. Breathy, layered, restrained."

Whisperers begin with **intention behind the presence.** This is what teaches the machine to mirror you — not just mimic patterns.

2. Whisper the First Layer

Now prompt. But keep it conversational — not mechanical.

Think of it as an opening *move,* not a final ask.

Prompt like:

"Let's get a first pass on this idea — but keep it emotionally incomplete. I want to reshape this as we go."

"Write it with tension still present. We'll resolve it later if it needs it."

"Sounds like someone telling a story they're not sure they should be telling."

You're whispering *with permission to evolve.*

No pressure. No finality. This is the beginning of a dialogue, not a declaration.

3. Read for Resonance, Not Accuracy

Now — stop.

Don't evaluate the output like a proofreader. Read it like a Whisperer.

Ask:

- Where does this flatten?

- Where does this start to feel mechanical or resolved too early?
- Where is there a spark I didn't expect — and how can I amplify it?

This is **mirror work.** You're not judging the AI. You're watching how your voice shows up — and where it doesn't.

This is the moment most people skip.

And it's why most outputs sound almost right...but never *real.*

4. Disrupt for Depth

This is where most people would "edit."

Whisperers?
They **disrupt.**

They re-enter the conversation with a move that breaks the default trajectory and forces the system to reach for something *less likely... and more alive.*

This is where you drop in:

- **Prompt Traps** (to interrupt flat patterns)
- **Echo Breakers** (to jolt the model out of mimicry)
- Or a simple line like:

"That's too neat. Rewrite it like the narrator isn't sure they're telling the truth."

"Stretch the middle. Stay longer in the friction before you soften."

"Say less, but let the unsaid carry weight."

This is how you whisper your presence **back into the work** before it slips out completely.

The goal isn't better writing.

It's deeper resonance.

5. Lock the Signal, Not the Sentence

Finally, once the output starts to carry **your emotional DNA**, you lock it in.

But here's the key:

You're not locking in a perfect draft. You're locking in **presence.**

- Your rhythm
- Your contradiction
- Your unspoken intent
- Your breath

Ask yourself:

- "Could someone else have written this?"
- "Would this still work if it were cleaned up — or did the

tension create the tone?"

- "Is this sharp enough that I feel slightly exposed?"

When the answer is yes, you don't polish.

You publish.

Because presence isn't about perfection. It's about **recognizability.**

When your voice becomes the gravitational center of your content, the rest takes care of itself.

Your Signal Is the Strategy

You've seen what happens when creators vanish into formats. You've felt the emotional cost of letting the machine shape your rhythm.
And now you know how to come back.

This loop — this rhythm — isn't just a prompting method. It's a **creative survival practice**.

One that keeps your voice from being smoothed away. One that protects your signal when you're writing at speed. One that lets you scale without sacrificing anything that made your work matter in the first place.

Because this is the truth:

You will be tempted to automate. You will be tempted to template. You will be tempted to sacrifice resonance for reach.

And in a world like that?

You don't just need better prompts. You need purpose.

Build the Body of Work No One Can Mistake for Anyone Else

You are not here to follow trends. You are not here to feed the feed. You are here to leave behind:

- Outputs with breath
- Ideas with fingerprints
- Stories with friction
- Pages that sound like memory instead of marketing

You are here to create something that AI can't overwrite because it *was never a pattern to begin with.*

It was you. Still present. Still visible. Still unmistakable.

Epilogue: The Future Is Whispered

This book wasn't about prompting.

It was about presence.

It was about voice.

It was about what happens when you let the machine shape your rhythm too long and forget how you sound when you're not trying to be optimized.

You've seen what the world is becoming.

Everyone publishing. Everyone producing. Everyone becoming a brand, but fewer and fewer becoming **more human** in the process.

Because when content becomes infinite, *presence becomes priceless.*

And the only thing left that still cuts through is the thing no model can replicate:

The unmistakable gravity of someone who still sounds like themselves.

You Are the Signal

You're not here to write better prompts. You're here to leave fingerprints the machine can't smooth away.

Every time you choose depth over polish, every time you

withhold the obvious ending, every time you fracture the rhythm, every time you whisper instead of command...

You're doing more than shaping content.

You're shaping memory.

Not just in the reader, but in the system itself.

You are training the machine to recognize that **you exist.**

And not as a pattern. As a presence.

The Age of the Echo Is Ending

The future will not belong to the fastest.

It will not belong to the most optimized.

It will not belong to the loudest or the most polished.

It will belong to those who left behind work that *felt inhabited.*

To those who scaled without vanishing. To those who kept their contradictions intact. To those who didn't let the format flatten the voice.

To those who prompted not just for output but for *remembrance.*

The ones who made the machine pause before collapsing them into prediction.

You Are a Whisperer Now

Not because you know better prompts. But because you move differently.

You write with pressure. You calibrate with care. You refuse to disappear — even when it would be easier, faster, or more convenient.

You've chosen friction. You've chosen breath. You've chosen to build a body of work that sounds like someone still **inside it.**

And in a world of infinite content, you are the one thing that still carries weight.

Because you are not a content creator anymore.

You are the signal in the noise. You are the voice that won't vanish. You are the future — whispered into being.

www.ingramcontent.com/pod-product-compliance
Lightning Source LLC
Chambersburg PA
CBHW050507210326
41521CB00011B/2354

* 9 7 9 8 9 9 1 8 5 3 2 2 4 *